University Teaching

University Teaching

A Guide for Graduate Students

Edited by

Leo M. Lambert
Stacey Lane Tice
Patricia H. Featherstone

With a Foreword by
Patricia Hutchings *and* Ellen Wert

Syracuse University Press

Copyright © 1996 by Syracuse University Press
Syracuse, New York, 13244-5160
All Rights Reserved

First Edition 1996
96 97 98 99 00 01 6 5 4 3 2 1

The paper used in this publication meets the minimum requirements of American National Standard for Information Sciences—Permanence of Paper for Printed Library Materials, ANSI Z39.48-1984. ∞™

This book was published with the assistance of a grant from the Pew Charitable Trusts.

Library of Congress Cataloging-in-Publication Data
University teaching : a guide for graduate students / edited by Leo M. Lambert, Stacey Lane Tice, Patricia H. Featherstone ; with a foreword by Patricia Hutchings and Ellen Wert.—1st ed.
    p. cm.
    Includes bibliographical references (p.   ) and index.
    ISBN 0-8156-2637-1 (pbk. : alk. paper).
    1. College teaching—United States. 2. Graduate students—United States. I. Lambert, Leo M. II. Tice, Stacey Lane.
III. Featherstone, Patricia H.
LB2331.U757   1995
378.1'25—dc20   95-32402

Manufactured in the United States of America

To the hundreds of graduate students at Syracuse University
with whom we have worked
and from whom we have learned so much.

Leo M. Lambert is associate vice chancellor and dean of graduate studies and professor of foundations of educational policy and practice at the University of Wisconsin–La Crosse. He was formerly associate dean of the graduate school and director of the TA Program at Syracuse University, where he founded the Future Professoriate Project, an effort supported by FIPSE and The Pew Charitable Trusts to provide prospective college and university faculty with more in-depth, discipline-based preparation in teaching under the guidance of senior faculty members. Dr. Lambert is also a member of the Advisory Board of Undergraduate Teaching Improvement Council of the University of Wisconsin System.

Stacey Lane Tice is assistant director of the TA Program of the Graduate School at Syracuse University where she supervises the day-to-day operations of the TA Orientation Program and year-round programming for the nearly 800 teaching assistants. She also works closely with Charles Watson on the Future Professoriate Project and Preparing Future Professors: A New York State Consortium Project which is sponsored by the Fund for the Improvement of Postsecondary Education (FIPSE). She is coeditor (with Leo M. Lambert) of *Preparing Graduate Students to Teach,* a book based on their national study of TA training programs and practices.

Patricia H. Featherstone is a Ph.D. candidate in the English Department of Syracuse University. At Syracuse she has taught writing studios, English literature courses, and a lab section of ENG 610, Oral Communication, a course for International TAs. In 1992 Patricia received an Outstanding TA Award. Currently, she is a graduate teaching consultant for the TA Program, where she is involved in a variety of projects that promote the preparation of graduate students for careers in the academy. She is also a member of the Syracuse University Assessment Coordinating Committee.

Contents

PART TWO

Enhancing Learning and Teaching

Foreword

As friends and long-time observers of teaching at Syracuse University, we are delighted to help launch this collection of essays about university teaching. Over the past few years especially, we have been fortunate to be part of Syracuse University's Future Professoriate Project, as a presenter at the Faculty Teaching Mentors Seminar [Hutchings] and as officer on a grant in support of the initiative [Wert].

The essays in this volume constitute a rich resource. You will find practical strategies to try in your own classrooms as well as gleanings from current research on teaching and learning. More importantly perhaps, this volume makes accessible what is too often private: the thinking of a diverse group of teachers about what they do and why and about the place of teaching in the lives and responsibilities of teachers at all points in their careers.

In this way, the essays also demonstrate that teaching is something that all of us learn about over time through ongoing reflection, conversation, and assessment. It is striking, in this regard, that the volume is coauthored by faculty and graduate students. This partnership reflects the growing interest, at Syracuse and on many campuses, in creating a culture of teaching in which colleagues work together on issues of teaching and its improvement. Making teaching a more collegial, public venture is an important step forward—one this volume will both reinforce and inform.

Finally, our pleasure in introducing this book has much to do, also, with our own experience as teachers of undergraduates. We know how helpful it is to have a sense of the larger context in which teaching and student learning take place. We also know how important it is, whether in your first or fiftieth semester of teaching, to have access to the ideas and insights of other teachers. This book offers both. It will be a great boon to teachers at all points in their careers, on campuses across the country.

We extend special thanks to Syracuse University for making this resource available. We hope that you will find it, as we do, an invitation to join a rich conversation about teaching, learning, and scholarship and that in time it will move you to contribute to this conversation yourself.

Patricia Hutchings
American Association for Higher Education

Ellen Wert
The Pew Charitable Trusts

Preface

One of the great sea changes occurring at leading research universities is a renewed dedication to the quality of undergraduate teaching. This phenomenon can be at least partially explained as a response to external publics. At state-supported universities, legislators bemoan the emphasis institutions place on research at the expense of undergraduate teaching. In the private sector, parents taking out a second mortgage to pay hefty tuition bills are examining more critically the value of private higher education. Nationally, in both sectors, a focal point of this discussion has been the use (and abuse) of graduate teaching assistants (TAs) to deliver undergraduate instruction. Syracuse University was one of the first major universities to develop, under the auspices of the TA Program of its Graduate School, a comprehensive summer orientation program for the more than 325 new teaching assistants appointed each year. The TA Program has expanded rapidly since 1987 and has grown to include a successful program of language instruction for TAs requiring assistance in improving their proficiency in spoken English, an awards program for outstanding TAs, and a series of academic year colloquia and professional development seminars focusing on teaching and professional life in the academy.

Syracuse University made even greater strides in 1991 by launching the Future Professoriate Project, with the aid of $1 million from the Fund for the Improvement of Postsecondary Education of the U.S. Department of Education and The Pew Charitable Trusts. The Future Professoriate Project is dedicated to preparing graduate students for academic careers by combining graduate study's traditional emphasis on excellence in scholarship with opportunities for a discipline-based, advanced teaching apprenticeship (termed a teaching associateship) under the careful guidance of a faculty teaching mentor. Teaching associates also have the opportunity to participate in an array of discipline-based professional development seminars hosted by their home departments. In simple terms, the goal of the project is to prepare aspiring faculty members to excel in both research and teaching, and, whenever possible, to help them understand the connectedness of all facets of their professional lives.

The idea for this volume was born out of the Syracuse University experience in preparing graduate students for successful classroom, laboratory, and studio experiences with undergraduate students. Other respected volumes of readings about teaching have previously been distributed to new TAs upon their arrival at Syracuse, but we believe that this book, authored by Syracuse University faculty and graduate students, offers the advantage of several important underpinnings:

• First, the chapter topics stem from ongoing, intellectually rigorous conversations about teaching that regularly happen on the Syracuse campus, involving both professors and graduate students. From your very first day as a new teaching assistant, we encourage you to be an active and thoughtful contributor to these conversations.

• Second, we believe that good teachers are reflective teachers, i.e., that they are continually engaged in a process of self-examination with the ultimate aim of improving student achievement, whether they have twenty-five days or twenty-five years of experience. We trust that the chapters in this volume will provide you with useful ideas and techniques as you begin your always-unfolding journey as a reflective teacher.

• Third, the many contributors to this book encourage you to think expansively about teaching. Becoming a good teacher is not about just becoming a better public speaker and learning to organize a course syllabus and lecture notes (although these certainly are valuable skills). Good teaching also means knowing your students as learners and appreciating the diverse perspectives they bring with them to the classroom. We hope you will come to appreciate, as we have, that some of the most rewarding moments in teaching occur outside formal classroom meetings, during office hours and one-on-one tutorials. And, we want to challenge you to experiment with your teaching. Try incorporating writing assignments in your classes to promote active learning; have your teaching videotaped and then ask a faculty mentor or peer to sit with you to constructively critique a class session; or try new approaches to assessing how much your students are actually learning in your class, laboratory, recitation section, or studio. In our view, these are some of the broader activities that contribute to a more complete definition of good teaching.

Above all, we want you to know that we appreciate what a difficult job it is to manage the juggling act of being a graduate student and a teacher with other life interests and responsibilities. This will undoubtedly be one of the most demanding periods of your life, but we trust that you will also look back upon this as one of the most joyful and rewarding. I wish you great success as you enter the classroom this fall. Welcome to the fellowship of teaching.

Syracuse, New York   Leo M. Lambert

Acknowledgments

Our editorial work could never have been brought to successful fruition without the aid and expertise of many good friends and colleagues. We thank Bry Pollack of the American Association for Higher Education and Professor Bill Cerbin of the University of Wisconsin–La Crosse for reviewing the entire manuscript and offering many helpful suggestions. Annette Salsbery and Kelly Salsbery of Syracuse University worked diligently under great time pressures to prepare a test edition of the manuscript for use during the August 1994 TA orientation program at Syracuse University. Our colleagues in the TA Program at Syracuse, Chuck Watson, Donna Hayes, and Victoria Landers, ably assisted us with our other obligations to the Graduate School while we were engaged with this project.

We owe a special thanks to our good colleagues and friends Pat Hutchings of the American Association for Higher Education (AAHE) and Ellen Wert of The Pew Charitable Trusts not only for writing the foreword to this volume but also for sustaining and enriching the quality of the campus dialogue about teaching and learning at Syracuse University. The support of AAHE and The Pew Charitable Trusts has been vital in advancing the efforts of Syracuse University to prepare graduate students as future members of the professoriate.

Our greatest thanks, of course, are to our faculty and graduate student collaborators on this project. Over the past eight years we have spent hundreds of delightful hours with faculty and graduate student colleagues discussing and debating how to best help graduate students learn the craft of university teaching. In his landmark book, *Scholarship Reconsidered: Priorities of the Professoriate*, Ernest Boyer reminds us that "teaching, at its best, means not only transmitting knowledge, but *transforming* it and *extending* it as well." This volume represents our best efforts to transform and extend knowledge about preparing graduate students for their important undergraduate teaching roles in American universities.

We dedicate this volume to the hundreds of graduate students at Syracuse University with whom we have worked and from whom we have learned so much.

Syracuse, New York   Leo M. Lambert
January 1995   Stacey Lane Tice
                                               Patricia H. Featherstone

Contributors

Salma Abu Ayyash is a Ph.D. student in electrical and computer engineering and a teaching associate at Syracuse University. A TA since 1992, she has taught a variety of classes and was one of the group who initiated the Future Professoriate Project in her department.

Kristi Andersen, a professor of political science, has been a faculty member in the Political Science Department at Syracuse University since 1984, where she has also served as director of graduate studies.

Mary Cannella is a Ph.D. candidate in electrical and computer engineering and a teaching associate at Syracuse University. She is currently participating in her department's initialization of the Future Professoriate Project.

Wynetta Devore is professor of social work at Syracuse University. Professor Devore joined the School of Social Work faculty in 1980 following appointments at Kean College and Rutgers University. She is coauthor of *Ethnic-Sensitive Social Work*, now in its third edition, and articles about ethnic-sensitive practice and practice with African-American populations.

Marvin Druger is professor of biology and science education and chair of the Department of Science Teaching at Syracuse University. He has received numerous awards for science teaching and was a Fulbright lecturer at the University of Sydney, Australia (1969–70) and a visiting Fellow at the Western Australian Institute of Technology.

Jerry Evensky, a professor of economics, has been a member of the Economics Department of Syracuse University since 1985. He loves to teach and do research and would be unhappy in any job that didn't encourage, nurture, and reward excellence in both these pursuits.

Katalin Fabian is a Ph.D. student in the Political Science Department at Syracuse University, where she has been a teaching associate.

Michael Flusche is associate vice chancellor for academic affairs and associate professor of history at Syracuse University. He has taught a variety of courses, from the two-semester survey of American history, to honors seminars on creative approaches to problem solving. He coordinated the faculty committee that established the assessment program at Syracuse University.

Bethany Heaton-Crawford is assistant director of the Center for Academic Achievement and Coordinator of Learning Disability Services for Syracuse University. She is a certified rehabilitation counselor and has worked at the center at Syracuse University for the past three years.

Jane Hendler is a Ph.D. candidate in the Department of English at Syracuse University. As a teaching assistant, she has taught courses in nineteenth- and twentieth-century American literature, as well as courses for the writing program and "Oral Communication in Teaching," a course for international teaching assistants. She has been a teaching fellow for three years.

Sharon Hollenback is professor of public communication at the S. I. Newhouse School of Public Communication of Syracuse University and heads the undergraduate television-radio-film writing program there. She also teaches courses in TV and film criticism, broadcast writing, screenwriting, and social-cultural-political effects of the media, and she is an active contributor to the honors program at the University.

Eric Howes is a teaching resource expert in the Middle School of the West Genesee School District in Syracuse, New York. Previously, he taught for three years in the Landmark School of Beverly, Massachusetts, and earned his M.A. in learning disabilities from Syracuse University, where he was a graduate assistant for Learning Disability Services.

R. David Lankes is a Ph.D. student in the School of Information Studies at Syracuse University with an interest in wide area networking and multimedia distribution. He has a background in computing and system administration as well as visual and conceptual design. He is a cofounder of the AskERIC Project, which seeks to bring educators innovative use of the Internet.

Ian Lapp is a Ph.D. candidate in sociology at the Maxwell School of Citizenship and Public Affairs of Syracuse University. He has done research and taught courses on the intersection of race, class, and gender, and his passion for teaching has earned him an outstanding teaching assistant award and an appointment as teaching associate.

Lawrence J. Lardy is professor of mathematics and a faculty member of the Mathematics Department at Syracuse University since 1964. He served as chair of the department from 1982–88 and has been a participant in the department's implementation of the Future Professoriate Project.

Kenneth J. Lindblom is a Ph.D. student in the Department of English at Syracuse University. He is also a teaching associate in the writing program, a teaching fellow, and a recipient of the outstanding TA award. His articles on teaching have appeared in *College English, English Journal,* and the *English Record.*

Judy Long is professor of sociology at Syracuse University and has previously taught at the University of Chicago and Cornell University. She is author of *Telling Women's Lives: Subject/Narrator/Read/Text* (1994) and has also written numerous articles for professional journals.

Michael Lynch is an assistant professor of philosophy at the University of Mississippi. He earned his Ph.D. from Syracuse University. In the summer of 1993, he received a grant to rewrite the *Instructor's Manual for PHI 187,* a guidebook for graduate students teaching an introductory course for the first time.

Tracy Mannara is a Ph.D. student in electrical and computer engineering and a teaching associate at Syracuse University. She has spent three of her five years at Syracuse University teaching a variety of laboratories in the Bioengineering and Electrical engineering departments.

Milene Morfei is a Ph.D. student in psychology at Syracuse University where she has been a teaching fellow for three years and winner of an outstanding TA award. Previously, she served as acting assistant dean of students at Wells College.

Frederick Phelps is professor of electrical and computer engineering and directs the Iconic Communication Laboratory in the College of Engineering at Syracuse University. An engineering educator for more than 25 years, he has taught at Case Western Reserve University and at the Claremont Colleges before coming to Syracuse. He currently serves on the active learning task force and also offers a graduate course in teaching engineering.

Mary K. Porter is a Ph.D. candidate in mathematics and a teaching associate at Syracuse University. She has taught college mathematics for nine years, including one year as a full-time instructor at Hobart and William Smith Colleges. She is presently doing research on the learning and teaching of college mathematics.

Emily Robertson is associate professor in cultural foundations of education and philosophy at Syracuse University. Her research in the philosophy of education focuses on moral perception and judgment and the capacities for critical reflection.

Duane H. Roen is currently at Arizona State University. He was formerly professor of writing and English at Syracuse University. He is the coauthor of *Becoming Expert: Thinking and Writing Across the Curriculum*, a book that encourages students to take responsibility for their own learning.

Ruth V. Small is associate professor and director of the master of library science program at Syracuse University and teaches courses in the School of Information Studies which explore the many aspects of information presentation. She has designed, developed, and evaluated computer-based educational and training programs in a variety of settings and has also written a number of journal articles and book chapters.

Robert Van Gulick is professor of philosophy and director of the cognitive science program at Syracuse University. He also serves as director of undergraduate studies for the Philosophy Department and as secretary-treasurer of the Society for Philosophy and Psychology.

Barbara Walter is associate professor of art in the College of Visual and Performing Arts at Syracuse University. She teaches three-dimensional problem solving and metalsmithing for the School of Art. Her mechanical jewelry pieces have been exhibited nationally and internationally and the Victoria and Albert Museum in London purchased a piece for their collection.

Charles Widener is currently in the School of Education at Syracuse University pursuing a teaching degree. He has a B.S.W. and an M.S.W. from Syracuse University and has been a teaching assistant for four years.

Zeus Yiamouyiannis is a Ph.D. candidate in cultural foundations of education at Syracuse University. He is particularly interested in involving students' expertise in the production of their own knowledge. He likes to use cooperative and inclusive strategies in the classroom to evoke discussion and student participation and to help students acquire skills and ideas that may be unfamiliar.

PART ONE

University Teaching

1

Practical Tips for Teaching at the University Level

MARVIN DRUGER

You first few classes are especially important because this is when an instructor sets the stage for the rest of the semester. Many students feel insecure in the first class session. They wonder: What is the class all about? What sort of person is the instructor? What does he expect of me? Is she sympathetic to my needs and interests? Does he realize that I want to learn but that I am no genius? Is this class going to be boring? How well will I relate to her? Will there be many assignments? How will I be evaluated? What type of exams will he give? How well does she know the subject matter? Can he explain the material well and answer my questions? If needed, can I get extra help from her?

Because most students have questions like these at the beginning of the course, you should be prepared at the first session to provide answers to at least some of them and to establish a good learning atmosphere. To this end, I offer some strategies and tips that I have found useful during my forty years of teaching at the college level.

Expect to be worried or nervous. Feeling some tension can help motivate you to put extra effort into your teaching and do a more effective job. But remember, your students probably feel more insecure and uncomfortable than you do, and it's not unusual for the first class session to be a silent, tense occasion as students anxiously await the answers to their questions. You have the advantage of being in command of the situation. Set the direction and take the initiative to establish expectations and a good learning atmosphere.

Prepare thoroughly. It is particularly important that you know the

3

subject matter you will be dealing with during your first couple of class meetings. Write yourself an outline specifying objectives, key concepts, and questions to ask the students. Especially plan, in detail, the strategy you will use for teaching that first class session. Students can sense an instructor's insecurity and lack of preparation. They likely will test you during the first few class sessions to establish for themselves whether or not you know the material. Make them confident in your subject matter competency, and you will have taken a major step forward in establishing a positive learning environment.

Tell the students who you are. Write your name on the board and tell the students something about your background and special interests. A complete autobiography is not necessary, but you do want students to know that you are a real person, not just a talking statue.

Tell the students as much as you can about the course objectives and how you will conduct the class. Tell them about assignments, exams, grading, class procedures, and your expectations of them as learners. Allow for flexibility in your organization of the course. Let students know that you are receptive to suggestions and criticisms and that you are willing to change course procedures when changes seem reasonable. The essence of your approach should be to make your students aware that your procedures are intended to facilitate their learning.

Inform students about any special rules or policies. Be clear about your attendance policy, the rules about handing in late assignments and making up missed exams, and other procedures. Stating your expectations clearly and early in the course usually will bring about the behavior you desire.

When you establish a policy or a special procedure, explain its rationale to your students. Explain how the policy or procedure will help facilitate their learning. Students usually will be more reasonable in their thinking than you might imagine.

Explain exams, grading, and other evaluation procedures very clearly. Grades are obviously of great interest to students. Tell them exactly how their final grade will be decided. Then keep the students informed at all times during the semester about their progress and grade status.

Design your exams and assignments to be consistent with your objectives. Students study in relation to how you test them. If you tell students that your tests will require problem solving and thinking, they will study accordingly. However, if instead you test for recall and memory, they will study by memorizing the material.

Be professional in your manner. Demonstrate to your students that you expect to do work in class. Treat students with respect and they will react in the same manner.

Assign some work to be handed in at the next class session. Get the students involved in the course right away. This assignment is an indication that you mean business and that you want the students to learn as much as possible. Grade that first assignment with special care and thoroughness and return it at the next class meeting, with feedback that will allow for improvement in the next assignment. Use the opportunity to set the tone for future assignments. The students will know what your expectations are and that you take the time to review their work carefully. This is also a good time to reinforce the policy that you expect assignments to be handed in on time and that you will read and return them promptly.

Be cautious of dismissing your class early. Students are entitled to a full class session. Prepare extra material for each session, just in case you have a few minutes left at the end of the class. It is important to let your students know that there is much interesting material for them to learn and that you will provide the opportunity for them to interact with that material for the full class session. Students will quickly come to expect a full session each time.

Plan a motivating beginning, a middle core, and an ending for each class session. Try to introduce the subject matter by relating it to the students' experiences and backgrounds. Why would they want to know about this topic? What does it mean to them? Next, deal with the core material by lecture, discussion, demonstration, question and answer. Finally, summarize the main points to tie the whole session into an integrated whole. What are the few essential "nuggets" that you want students to take with them from the class session? These nuggets should transcend the details of the class and serve instead as organizers to help the students recall details.

Learn the names of your students as soon as possible. One helpful procedure is to have your students fill out index cards, indicating their backgrounds, interests, career goals, and any other information that will help you get to know them as learners. In class refer to the students by name, and you will be surprised at the good rapport that results.

Be available to students. Requiring that students sign up for scheduled conference hours is an effective procedure for encouraging students to talk to you. The usual approach of "drop in any time" or "see me during office hours" rarely brings to your office students who need assistance or who would like to chat.

Vary your teaching strategies. Don't spend the entire class session lecturing. Sometimes lecturing is appropriate and effective, but it is an approach that should be used sparingly. If you always lecture, then students will fall into the pattern of being completely passive in class. They will sit like lumps, simply writing down what you say without their thinking; then, just before exams, a frantic search will begin to find out "What did the instructor mean by this sentence?" For students to understand involves brain reactions from them, and their brain reactions can be stimulated by their oral participation in class. So, stop frequently and ask questions. Then be patient. Wait at least seven to ten seconds for the students to respond; the longer you wait, the better quality response you are likely to receive. Try to draw answers from a variety of students, to maximize discussion and interaction. If you get students involved in questions and discussion during your first few class sessions, they will come to expect, and enjoy, this pattern of involvement. Later in the course, you can use lecturing more often without losing your students' active involvement and interest. Remember, students are not empty vessels to be filled with information. Your task is to stimulate effective learning.

Don't feel that you have to know all the answers. If you overprepare your lessons and try to have an excellent grasp of the subject matter, you likely will be able to answer most questions students come up with. However, students need to realize that you are human and that you don't have all the answers. Sometimes you might just forget an answer; other times you simply might not know the answer. In such cases, if you attempt to hedge your response, it will soon become painfully obvious to your students that you do not know what you are talking about, and their faith in you will decline rapidly. There are a variety of ways this situation can be effectively confronted. You could admit "I don't know," or suggest a reference, or ask a student to look up the answer, or volunteer to look up the answer yourself, or refer the question back to the class. Saying "I don't know" is perfectly appropriate and realistic, but it should not be said so frequently that students become convinced that you really do not have a good command of the subject matter. Extra preparation and a good command of your subject matter will help avoid this situation.

Be encouraging to students. Sometimes it takes courage for a student to offer a comment during class. If you sneer at an answer or make a sarcastic remark, that student might never again participate in class. Students are especially sensitive to your words, actions, and responses to their behavior. Your sarcastic remark could be perceived as a personal affront. So, think twice when responding to a student, and be sensitive. Your positive response will encourage a positive counterresponse. Praise good work. Think and act in a positive manner. An occasional "nice work," "great idea," or "good question" can bring out the best in students. A comment such as "that's a dumb question" has no place in the learning environment.

It is especially important to be encouraging during the first few classes, when students are trying to establish a rapport with you. You want them to learn to feel comfortable asking questions and be actively involved in class proceedings. Frequently, a student will have a question in mind but will not ask it for fear of appearing stupid, then someone else will ask that very question. The same "stupid" question might very well be in the minds of other students in the class. Perhaps it reflects a shared misunderstanding, or a step that you skipped, or an inadequate explanation. Oftentimes, a "stupid" question will be an indicator of how well you are teaching. So, you should handle all questions in a professional manner. If you feel that the question really should not be answered at the time it is asked—because of time constraints or its appropriateness—ask the student to see you later and move on.

Laugh a lot. Teaching should not be a grim encounter between you and your students. Laughing at your own mistakes emphasizes your human qualities, and students respond positively. A bit of humor does not destroy the seriousness of your lesson.

Don't expect every day of teaching to be filled with sunshine and roses. All you can do is your best, and sometimes that is a disaster. The reasons for disaster are not always clear. You might have been in a bad mood, the students might have been distracted preparing for an important exam in another course, the weather might be hot and humid. All these factors, and many others, can contribute to a disappointing class session. Everyone has bad days. Try to put them behind you and look to the future. The sun will soon reappear.

Teach for the future. Upon completion of your course, the students should have a positive attitude about the course and the subject matter, a feeling of accomplishment, an awareness of the scope of the subject, knowledge about how to learn more about it, and a set of experiences that contributed to their personal growth. You can add more objectives to this list, but the ultimate effect of your teaching and your course will be manifested many years after its completion when details of its content are long forgotten. Teach with these long-term future effects in mind.

The large questions. Having presented the preceding very practical tips, I would like to pose some questions that merit your thoughtful consideration. Why do we teach the content we teach? Why do we lecture so much? Why don't more instructors think about teaching from a learner's perspective? Why don't we specify objectives in behavioral terms? Why do we insist on teaching students, instead of guiding and motivating them to learn on their own? Why are examinations so variable in equity? Why don't we try to learn more about our strengths and weaknesses as instructors? What are the most important outcomes of a college education? What will students gain from their college education? What do we as instructors do to build self-confidence, a positive attitude toward learning, motivation to learn more, sufficient background to know how to learn more in the field, and practical skills that will transfer to our students' everyday lives?

These are some of the large questions I ask myself periodically. Despite years of experimentation with teaching strategies and continual updating of my course materials, I still find these questions to be the ones that cause me to reflect on my current practice and inevitably to make changes. Ideally, you will identify your own set of large questions that you periodically will analyze and respond to in light of your current practice. As we reflect on our practices, we are very likely to be more successful in encouraging student learning.

2

The Lecture

JERRY EVENSKY

General Thoughts On Lecturing

Defining Terms: Understanding versus Learning

I begin by defining terms because communication, be it on paper or in a lecture hall, depends on a common language and a common understanding about what the words mean. I will use the terms *understand* and *learn* as I explain my view of lecturing. Given that we may not share a common meaning, it is imperative that you know what I mean by these terms.

By *understand,* I mean to appreciate correctly the meaning of a concept (a term or an idea) or the logic of a weave of concepts when presented. By *learn,* I mean to master a concept or the logic of a weave of concepts so that you can independently call upon and successfully apply those tools as needed. As I define these terms then, understanding is a prerequisite for learning. You can watch and listen to a lesson on bike riding and understand how to ride a bike, but that won't be sufficient to get you down the block and back on your new ten speed. To move from understanding to learning requires that you take what you understand and practice, practice, practice with it.

When I lecture about how, all else held constant, a change in German real interest rates can affect the strength of the dollar relative to the mark, I want my students to understand the terms involved and the weave of logic that ties these terms into a story about interest rates, international capital flows, and exchange rates. I want my students to understand, but I do not expect them to learn this logic in the course of my lecture. To take their understanding and make it learning, they must practice: they must do homework that requires them to apply the tools they understand to some contrived or real events I present; they must read the newspaper and apply what they understand to analyze the flow of real events; they must prepare for my exams on which they know I will ask them to analyze real or contrived events.

I tell my students about this distinction—understanding versus learning—the first day of every semester because I want them to recognize our respective responsibilities. My primary job is to ensure that they understand the material. I tell them: "If the thread breaks, I need to know so I don't go on without you." Their job is to learn the material. That requires them to do two things: ask if they don't understand, and practice, practice, practice. I assist them in their job by trying to create a classroom atmosphere that encourages questions and by providing practice tools (e.g., homework) and incentives (e.g., graded assignments). But I also try to make it clear that if they are to learn we must *both* do our jobs well.

The Value of Lecturing

A lecture allows you to exercise tight control over the teaching environment. You can talk as much or as little as you please, taking questions or inviting comments when and if you please. This control allows you to maintain the continuity of your presentation as it unfolds and to keep the focus of the students on the flow of the logic you seek to convey. Given this control, the great strength or value of a lecture format is that it allows you to convey efficiently and effectively the logic of a weave of terms and ideas.

The terms and ideas are the pieces you work with, and the story into which you weave them is the whole you create. As with the terms *understanding* and *learning,* I spend time on the first day of my course explaining my view of the relationship between the pieces and the whole. A metaphor I use to make this point is a puzzle. In a puzzle box are many pieces of information about an image. Any one of them gives very little information about that image. The image only unfolds as the pieces take their places in relation to one another; so, too, the pieces in your lecture course. Every piece of information is part of an image. The logic that unfolds in your lectures should make that image clear.

Many students are used to approaching their education as an exercise in the assimilation of pieces of information often by rote memory. But if they only learn the pieces as pieces, the image will never unfold for them. You have to work hard to keep them conscious of the big picture so that they will see the pieces as parts of a larger image. Only then will they be able consistently to take what they understand about the pieces and place them appropriately into a larger frame—that mind's eye image, that vision you want to share. Whether the content of the course is an image of how to approach a text or of how to analyze a capitalist economy or of the nature of chaos, a lecture format can be a very effective medium for communicating complex images efficiently and effectively.

Memorization is the lowest order of learning. The beauty of a lecture is that it offers you the opportunity to show your students how all the pieces can be arranged to produce a level of understanding (and, subsequently, learning) that is much greater than the simple sum of its parts.

The Micro and Macro of a Lecture: Class Culture and Individual Diversity

If there are 100 students in your lecture, then there are 102 personalities in the room. There are those 100 students who walk in bringing 100 different persons to this new setting, there is you and the person you are, and there is the class. Anyone who has taught for any length of time knows that the class, the wholeness of the 101 persons in the room, takes on an identity of its own. It develops a personality, a culture. As the leader of the class, you have a responsibility to be sensitive to the fact that each person in your class is unique, and you have an obligation to shape the culture of the class such that it is a constructive learning environment for every student in the class.

Creating a Constructive Class Culture

Respect. Your students expect and deserve to be treated with respect. And so do you. Treat them with respect, and insist that you and all fellow students be treated likewise. Remember, however, that there are levels of respect. Being treated with the basic respect one is due as a human being, as a teacher, or as a student should be automatic. But, respect as a good person, as a good teacher, or a good student is not and should not be automatic. Such respect is earned by the quality of performance.

Basic human respect is the foundation of all constructive human interaction, and thus it is a prerequisite for developing that earned respect that comes with a quality performance. If you want to nurture those performances, you must create that foundation. As with much of the culture creation that goes into a good classroom environment, if you make an effort to create that foundation, you will have the valuable and significant weight of student peer pressure on your side. The vast majority of students want to function in such an environment and will support your efforts to create it. But you must take the lead. A specific way to establish an atmosphere of respect is to establish community standards for classroom courtesy.

Courtesy. In a lecture setting, the close proximity of so many people trying to hear and follow your presentation makes everyone vulnerable to the discourtesies of any one person among them. The vast majority of students understand this and act responsibly; a few do not understand, a few do not care, and some have lapses of understanding or caring. Thus, if the lecture hall is going to be a constructive environment for all participants, it is important that you establish simple, clear community standards of behavior early and that you make clear your expectation for everyone to honor those standards. Also make it clear that you intend to enforce those standards. In the "Notes" section of my syllabus, for example, I have the following standards set forth for class courtesy:

• Late arrival should be an exception. When necessary, sit on entering side; do not disturb class.

• Early departure should be an exception. Only in an emergency or with prior consultation.

• Early preparation for departure—please don't.

• Talking—with everyone or with no one.

On the first day of class, I explain these standards and why I think they are important. I ask that they be honored. I find that the vast majority of the students not only happily honor the standards but they also appreciate them. In most cases, social pressure from the students themselves serves as enough of a sanction to enforce the standards.

On those rare occasions when social pressure is insufficient to enforce the standards, I do so. Initially I try subtle pressure—a look that makes eye contact but is not intended to embarrass. (I always avoid embarrassing someone. Doing so might affect the sense of security other students have about asking questions.) If that doesn't get the student's attention, I will try a more direct look, or even a closer physical presence, until the student realizes I want the offending behavior to stop. Those methods usually work; but failing that, I would stop the student after class and discuss the issue of community standards and being welcomed in the class.

In cases where there is a general lapse in courtesy (e.g., shuffling papers for early departure), I will stop and let the silence speak. And if the silence is not loud enough, I will briefly review the community standard of courtesy. That usually works.

Expect an Appropriate Level of Maturity from Your Students. Adhering to a set of community standards on courtesy is one way in which you set a standard for maturity in your lecture course. Another is embodied in the standards that are implicit in the way you talk and act with your students. If you talk and act with them as mature people of their age, they are more likely to respond to you as a mature person of their age. Don't underestimate your students' capacity for maturity.

Believe in Your Students. A necessary condition for success in a lecture class (or any class) is that you believe that your students can succeed, want to succeed, and are willing to work for success. Contrary to what some cynics would suggest, the vast majority of students do not object to hard work (which is not to say they like it). What they object to is hard busywork. Homework with no feedback, readings that never connect to the flow of the logic presented in lecture, or lectures with no logic make students wonder: "Why am I doing this?" If the class progresses and that "Why" is never resolved, then the "Why" becomes "Why bother?"

I believe that most students prefer a challenging class that teaches them something to a "blow-off" class that does not, even if the latter offers an easier grade. The vast majority of students value their education as much as anything else in life.[1] So, be demanding. Expect

---

1. How do I know this to be true? I do a "discovery" exercise early in the class related to decision rules (the algorithm we follow to make choices). The exercise involves a list of twenty-six characteristics students may choose to have (e.g., strength, beauty, charm, intelligence, wit, courage). In the first iteration of the exercise, I tell the students that each unit of every characteristic costs a dollar (obviously they have to conceptualize units themselves), and I give them a $100 "budget" to spend. I tell them that when they are finished spending their budget, they should put "Optimal" at the top of the column in which they listed their allocation of funds and then check the two items on which they spent the most. The first time I did this, as a lark I went down the list asking who spent the most on this or that. The students and I were struck that the overwhelming majority of the class had purchased more "intelligence" than anything

much of your students. Then show them you care by making the class worthwhile and by helping them to succeed.[2]

When students enter your class, their education becomes your and their shared responsibility. You should want to do the best you can to ensure that they leave with something worth the effort you expect of them. Expect them to make that effort. If they do, they deserve a benefit. I believe that is all most students want—worthwhile challenge.

Diversity: A Challenge and an Opportunity

Every student is unique, but you will be lecturing to all at once. That fact presents you with significant challenges and opportunities.

Diversity as a Challenge. The challenge of diversity lies in the fact that a lecture course can only be effective if the students have in common at least those skills and that knowledge base essential for understanding the content of your course. For example, if you are lecturing in English, your students must all understand English—and in particular the "English" you will be speaking. How do you address the challenges of diversity?

Prerequisite Skills. A lecture (or any class) can only be effective if the students have at least some essential skills in common. In the jargon of education these are prerequisite skills. In most classes these skills relate to language if we define language broadly to include mathematics. You are going to speak a language and if the students are going to "get it," they must speak that language too. If you have

---

else. In subsequent semesters I repeated the query, and the results have been very consistent. Now I use that empirical result to demonstrate the predictive power of empirical analysis. After they are done allocating, I predict the result. I have a perfect prediction record to date.

2. The last year I taught at a junior high school, my colleague Tom Franey and I tried an experiment. We took all the students who were entering the seventh grade with a reading level below second grade level and put them into a two-hour block (social studies and English). We worked those students very hard. They complained constantly. But we believed they could learn to read, we challenged them to do it, and they did. The gain was, on average, more than two reading levels. The result wasn't magic. Instead of being labeled "stupid" and facing low expectations, we called them "capable" and had high expectations—and we worked them very hard. When it was over, there was a sense of pride in our class and in each of those students that I've never seen in any other class. They didn't like the hard work, but they did appreciate it.

any doubt about your students' ability to speak your language, you must find a way to address this potential problem.

Identify the skills students will need to understand the presentation you plan to give (e.g., do they need to know basic geometry?). If these skills are not in place, your students will think you are speaking "Greek." Ask yourself the following questions: Is it safe to assume that these skills are in place? Do I know the audience well enough to answer this? When in doubt on either question, err on the side of caution. Any issue of this type should be addressed at the very beginning of a course, before students get locked into a schedule. If the size of the problem is unknown but the significance is potentially great, then either assume it's a big problem or come up with a rough-and-ready way to do a quick assessment. Do not assume it away because you want to ignore it.

If you assume or determine that there is a big prerequisite skills problem (a significant number of students have a deficit), you have two constructive choices. You can change the nature of your presentation to avoid the problem, or you can do some kind of readiness activity to bring students up to speed: e.g., textbook work, or practice with graphics, or start the course with a skills review. This last solution is particularly useful if the problem is broad (involving many students) but not deep (the skills involved are easily acquired). If the problem is small in scope (a few students) but deep, you can try to bring these students up to speed with out-of-class activities (e.g., a skill review workbook) or you can redirect them to a more appropriate course.

Be aware of the cultural location from which you derive your tacit knowledge. Besides differences in skills, an important source of diversity among your students is that their cultural backgrounds are plural. The less homogenous your class, the more significantly the tacit knowledge that comes from culture will affect your ability to communicate and relate your subject to your students. If your examples and language are drawn from your formative years in Kenya, then your students whose cultural understandings were formed in Iceland may not understand you. Conversely, if you grew up in Iceland . . .

You can't know the unique cultural understandings of every student in your class, but being aware of your students' cultural diversity will prompt you to remember that diversity as you try to think of ways in which to communicate and relate the material to each of them.

Diversity as an Opportunity. The opportunity of diversity lies in the fact that the cultural diversity can be a source of creative engagement with your students. For example, when I teach about how advantages affect market outcomes (e.g., insider information can allow one to make a killing in the stock market), I use examples that exploit the socioeconomic consequences of diversity: market power based on gender or race (e.g., "good ol' boy" networks or apartheid). Doing this makes the reality of diversity an asset because it relates the content of the course to the diversity of society and in turn to the diversity (or lack of it) of my class.

The diversity of tacit knowledge among my students (often culturally shaped) can be a source of intriguing interpersonal examples. For instance, in the process of developing a model of personal choice, I ask my students what they think is the probability of getting AIDS from one occasion of unsafe sex with a stranger. I rattle off successively higher probabilities and ask them to raise their hands when I get to the number they have in their head. Not surprisingly, the numbers vary. I use this fact to drive home the role of the variation of individuals' risk perceptions in explaining the variation of individuals' choices in apparently similar circumstances. (*Ceteris paribus,*—the higher the risk the lower the value of the choice.)

Another twist on the issue of diversity is that, while there is diversity within your class, your students often have things in common that, as a group, set them apart from the larger social context. For example, most of them share the common aspects of life as socially active young adults. By tapping into these issues you can relate the material more closely to the lives your students live. I do this in my own class by relating the concepts I am dealing with to the AIDS epidemic (e.g., the risk and choice example cited above). This puts my subject into the heart of an issue of which they are all acutely aware.

The Lecture as an Active Learning Environment.

Active Learning and Self-Assessment

The value of the lecture format is the continuity of presentation that it affords. As you give a lecture, a weave of logic (the story) should unfold for your students. If that story is new and complex, as well as compelling and understandable, most of your students will want to get it. If your students are prepared and engaged, if you explain any new terms so that the language never becomes an obstacle, and if the thread of your logic is drawn through the presentation with care so that the students can follow it—all of your students will get it.

This is the ideal. The product of this ideal is a new dimension or domain of understanding for your students.

Unfortunately we do not live in an ideal world. In the last section I made the point that you cannot assume that your students are ready. You have to be proactive about insuring that your students are ready. But being ready is not sufficient to insure success. If students are going to understand and learn, they must also be engaged in the process as it unfolds. Engaged learning is active learning.

You should not think of the lecture as the passive period to be relieved by "now we're going to do active learning." For your lecture to be effective, the process has to be an ongoing active learning experience. Your students need to be intellectually engaged throughout the process, constantly reflecting on and assessing their understanding as the lecture unfolds because they need to be sure they are "with you" if they are going to "get it."

Inevitably, you will use a term that you take as tacit knowledge, but that some students don't know. Or, you will explain a term thoroughly, but some students won't get it. Or, the thread of your logic will break for some students.[3] If any one of these things occurs, the students who are left behind are lost for the rest of that topic, and all future topics that depend on it.

To avoid this waste and frustration (and path to failure), two things need to happen. Your students need to constantly self-assess their understanding of what you are presenting, and when they are confused they need to ask for a clarification. This, in turn, requires that your students recognize when they don't know what's going on,[4] and that they feel safe in asking a clarifying question. If your students don't understand and don't ask a clarifying question, you might well be lecturing but you are not communicating.

If your lecture is to succeed, your students must be constantly self-assessing their understanding of the concepts and the logic you

3. One reason this may occur is that there is indeed a gap in the logic you are presenting. The best, engaged students will point out flaws in your logic, which is a compliment to them and a service to you.

4. When I was a junior high student, our principal always used to tell us, "an intelligent man is one who knows what he doesn't know."

are presenting and asking clarifying questions when need be. I offer three suggestions on how to stimulate active learning and some general thoughts on how to encourage active learning.

Stimulating Active Learning

• *The "Get Your Money's Worth" Technique.* I pose questions to my class to get them to think about the concepts and logic I am presenting. Immediately after I pose a question but before I call on someone, I tell them:

> Now, whether you intend to raise you hand or not, think about how you would answer this question. Once you've thought about your answer, listen to the answer of the person I call on, and then to my response to that person—doing this will help you see whether you're 'getting it.' If you just sit there passively and listen to the process unfold, you really can't know whether you're getting it—you want your money's worth out of this class. You're going to be sitting here anyway during this exchange. Invest yourself in the process, be active with your mind, test yourself.

Obviously, after going through this whole speech (or a variation) many times, I begin to give an abbreviated version, but I always remind them to be active, be engaged. Then, I will pause long enough before I call on someone[5] to ensure that there is time to reflect on the question.[6]

5. A note on calling on students. You need not call on the first person who raises his or her hand. If that student is a very active participant and others have not been, it's perfectly legitimate to look elsewhere and even wait for other hands to come up. I do this often. I usually look at the person I'm going to pass up this time (I never do this unless I've already called on that person at least once already that day), and I'll say something along the lines of, "I appreciate your participation, but let me try to get someone else involved." Then I will turn to the rest of the class and say something like, "Now, I know you're out there, let's see a hand from someone who hasn't participated yet." It doesn't always work, but it does often; and the person I passed up is generally ready to participate the next time, so it doesn't seem to be off-putting.

6. An alternate way to stimulate the same active engagement is to follow probing questions with a pregnant pause, and then call on specific students randomly. If students know they are at risk of being called on, that is an incentive to stay on top of the situation. Indeed, it is also an incentive to make a preemptive strike by asking a clarifying question when they are confused. I personally don't use this method because it doesn't suit my style or the class atmosphere I want to create, but if done with skill and sensitivity, it can be a very valuable technique.

• *The "Try This" Technique.* This is a variation on the one above in which I specifically direct everyone to take out a piece of paper and a pencil and write down their answer to a question I pose. This is especially helpful for a graphical or a particularly crucial and complicated issue. Putting it down on paper is much more of a commitment to an answer (there it is in black-and-white), and thus it is much harder for students to fool themselves about the correctness of their understanding (e.g., for them to think: "Yeah, that's what I would have answered").

• *The Ten-Second Count.* I ask the students to reflect on their understanding of what I have just presented by asking: "Are there any questions?" Then I wait ten seconds. The important part of this method is not so much the question as the wait. This is a lesson I learned from a videotape of myself teaching.[7] In the videotape critique session, one of my colleagues pointed out that the time between my query "Are there any questions?" and the next word out of my mouth was hardly enough for students to raise a hand, much less reflect on whether they had a question. So, armed with that insight, I started counting to ten whenever I asked "Any questions?" I have been struck by how often a question doesn't come until I get to a count of seven or eight. "Any questions?" is an invitation to your students to reflect on what they understand. That process is undermined if you don't wait. If you do, it encourages reflection. As a side benefit, it sends a signal to your students that you really do want to help them understand. I tell my students about the ten-count discipline I try to impose on myself, and I'll joke about it if in my enthusiasm I go roaring off too fast (and realize it).

All three techniques are very efficient (they take very little time) and very effective (students get immediate in-context feedback on their understanding). But, knowing they don't understand is only the first step; students also need to formulate and ask clarifying questions if they are going to "get it."

Encouraging Active Learning

Your students are only going to be independently engaged in reflecting on their understanding of your lecture if they think that any confusion they identify will be addressed. This means they must

---

7. In the jargon this is called "micro-teaching." I highly recommend that kind of self-observation. It is very valuable to see yourself as others see you.

be able to form and must feel secure enough to ask clarifying questions. If you take care to create an atmosphere that insures the safety of asking questions, the iterative process of query and response will help them develop their ability to form the questions.[8]

So how do you create an atmosphere that encourages students to ask clarifying questions? My own style is to take any questions almost any time because I want to identify and address confusion as soon as possible. But while I take all questions, I don't necessarily take them immediately or answer them when I get them. If I want to delay a question, I will just offer a hand signal to communicate that, while I see the hand, I'm not ready yet because I want to finish my train of thought. If I take a question but don't want to answer it at that time, I might explain to the questioner that the question takes me in a direction I don't want to pursue as a class, but I would be happy to talk about it after class. Or, maybe I'll explain that we don't have the tools in place yet to address that question as maturely as we will in two weeks, so hold on to it and ask again. Or, maybe I'll say, "I don't know, but I'll try to find out."

On the first day of class I talk about questions. I tell my students that I want them to feel safe enough about asking questions so that by the end of the course they each will have raised their hand at least once. In a class of more than a hundred students, raising your hand can be quite intimidating, but I want to send them a signal that I am going to make it as safe as possible and I will do everything I can to encourage all to participate.

I don't see questions as slowing me down. On occasion, taking questions has indeed put me behind where I had hoped to be, but I understand that there is no point in getting to the end if I get there alone, and I can usually catch up to my original time line by doing a little less embellishing along the way. Sure, there is the occasional student who gets perpetually carried away and can slow down the group; but in that special case, I begin to defer more and more of that person's questions to after class. The class sees what is going on,

---

8. One of the advantages of insuring that students see the pieces (concepts) as a part of a whole (logic) is that conceptualizing the content of the lecture course in this way helps students form their clarifying questions. As the image unfolds, your students can begin independently to locate points of confusion (the essence of self-assessment) —missing pieces or pieces that don't seem to fit anywhere. And furthermore, they can begin to intuit for themselves those pieces you may have missed, based on the context of the gap.

so they don't take it as a sign that my philosophy toward questions in general is less accepting.

But that's my style. Yours can be different, and be as good or better. What matters is the following:

• You should offer your students some means to ask clarifying questions in fairly short order (before the unfolding logic goes too far beyond the point of confusion—for confusion tends to snowball).

• You should nurture the sense among your students that clarifying questions are very welcome (given whatever format you deem appropriate), will be addressed seriously, and will be treated with respect. The quickest way to shut down questions is to demean someone for asking one. It not only intimidates the questioner, it sends a message to all who watched the interaction that, "Yes, you, too, could be embarrassed: Just ask a question."

Treating clarifying questions with respect is necessary but not sufficient to encourage those questions. It is also important that you address such questions constructively. If your student asks a clarifying question that is so muddled you don't understand it, you then know the confusion is significant. If you sense that this point of confusion is deep and peculiar to this individual (a judgment that becomes more keen as you get to know the questioner and the class), that's an opportune time to use the "let's talk after class" response. However, if you sense that the question is representative of a more general confusion in the class (when in doubt, I err on the side of this presumption), the process of working through what is being asked usually helps clear up the confusion. If your student asks a question and you are not sure what she is asking, repeat it back to her so you can ensure that you are about to answer what has been asked.[9]

Once you've completed your answer, check in with the questioner. I explicitly ask: "Did I answer your question?" It is easy to presume your answer made sense; it made sense to you as you gave

9. An aside on language and communication. Several years ago, I mentored a Korean teaching assistant who had a very strong accent. His students complained. We did a quick in-course evaluation and identified two areas of greatest concern: he was hard to understand, and he wasn't answering their questions effectively. So we experimented. I asked him to repeat every question back to the student who asked it, followed by the query: "Is this your question?" Then I asked him to follow his answer with the "Did I answer your question?" line. This process had a dramatic effect. This TA, whose student ratings had been abysmal, was soon among the highly ranked. The problem was never language, it was communication. Once the communication was carefully attended to, the problem disappeared.

it. But you can't be sure unless you ask. Asking also sends a signal to your students.[10] It says, "I not only want to hear your questions, I want to respond to them effectively." If you ask and the answer is, "no, you didn't answer it," then you can either try again (if I am going to do that, I usually ask the student to reexpress the question in a different way), or you can use the "let me follow up on this with you after class" line.

You Too Need To Be an Active Learner

Even as your students are actively engaged in trying to understand the material, you need to be actively engaged in gauging their understanding of that material. You can probe for such understanding with the techniques for encouraging active learning cited above, but the most important source of feedback is the student-initiated communication. If you are successful in creating a safe environment, students will feel free to initiate communication, the most common form of which is the clarifying questions cited above. These questions are extremely valuable because they are a very important form of assessment of your performance, providing feedback on what the students are and are not getting. Other kinds of student initiated communication that are invaluable for assessing your own performance are student questions that are extrapolated from the logic you have offered or synthesis statements offered by students. Clearly, when your student can ask a question that correctly extrapolates or can make a statement that effectively synthesizes, that is a good indication that at least someone is "getting it." The same kind of culture that encourages clarifying questions will encourage these kinds of efforts by your students.

Preparing for a Lecture: Some General Thoughts

"What Am I Going to Cover?": Choosing Your Content

In order to decide what concepts, principles, practices, procedures, and logic you want to present, you should ask yourself: What is it I want my students to be able to do when they've learned what I

---

10. Such signals are very important ways to assure my students that I am committed to doing my job, helping them understand. If they feel that way, it gives them more of an incentive to do their job—the grunt work (practice, practice, practice) necessary to learn what they understand.

am going to present? In the jargon of education this is defining your "objectives." Such objectives can range in intellectual sophistication from very low order: "I want them to be able to define 'Margin';" to very high order: "I want them to be able to thoughtfully critique the assertion of some famous economists that the construction of social ethics can ultimately be derived from an analysis of individual utility maximization." Whatever your behavioral objectives, being explicit about them helps you determine what your content should be and makes the next step, organizing, much easier.

Once you've determined the content, you must organize the concepts, principles, practices, and/or procedures into a thought process that the students can recognize as coherent. In other words, you must draw the thread through the logic that connects all these elements. If your students can follow the thread of your logic, they are more likely to move beyond simple memorization to more complex understanding.

Choose a structure that suits your style and your objectives. There are various (not mutually exclusive) structures available: compare/contrast, concrete to abstract, simple to complex, classification hierarchy, familiar to unfamiliar. In most cases it is valuable to build in a review-preview-present-review process. This enhances the sense of a flow in your logic because the preview orients and the review contextualizes. These can be very brief—reading an outline that's on the board is a simple preview.

Getting Ready to Lecture

As you plan, decide what props are necessary or helpful (e.g., colored chalk, handouts, an overhead projector), and be sure to arrange for them. Many great lecture plans have fizzled as lectures when some essential prop fails ("Oh my God, the overhead bulb is out!").

Rehearse your lecture. Your rehearsal need only be as formal as will be useful. I find that the first time I present a lecture on any topic, a formal rehearsal, aloud, is useful. I try to do it in a mirror so I can see that I am keeping my eyes on my audience. If I have lectured on something many times, I just mentally walk through my presentation to tune up.

Rehearsal will help you locate any snags in the flow of your logic. It is also an opportunity to practice with your examples to ensure that they work properly and that you can present them easily (e.g., many is the graph that didn't come out as planned because it wasn't rehearsed). It adds polish. It bolsters your confidence. It's a good time to ensure that the props you will bring with you are arranged in a way that is consistent with your presentation (e.g., are overheads in the right order?) and to think about how you might arrange the board if you'll be using it.

When you arrive to present your lecture, check things out. Are the props you will need there (e.g., chalk, eraser, overhead) and do they work (e.g., bulb in the overhead)? Is the physical environment amenable to attention (e.g., temperature, noise, glare)? If not, can you make it better (open/close a window, pull a shade, suggest avoiding some seats, close a door)?

The Goal of Preparation

Your goal, as you prepare, is to feel as ready as you can and to avoid the paralysis of nervousness. At the beginning of any new lecture experience (a new topic or a new audience or both), you will probably feel some nervousness. I've taught the same introductory course for eight years. I wrote the book for the course. I know this course. And yet I still start every semester a bit nervous because I don't know this class yet, they don't know me, and I know I'll be trying new things. Feeling nervous is okay, even normal, as you close the preparation stage, poised to begin the presentation. The crucial thing is to prepare as well as you can so that you are confident you have done your homework. That confidence will get you started, and the fruits of your efforts will allow that confidence to build. Expect to be nervous sometimes, but prepare to be confident.

Presenting a Lecture: Some General Thoughts

Establish and Maintain Your Lines of Communication

There are a number of means of communication with your students. The most important one in a lecture setting is your voice. So, the first and foremost concern you should have with respect to maintaining lines of communication is "can they hear me?" On the first day of a course and any time thereafter when you have any reason to be in doubt, ask "can you hear me?"

Another important form of communication is eye contact. If you want the students to feel that you and they are in the same class, look at them. Scan, regularly making eye contact with as many people as you can, so that they know you know they are there. Students appreciate feeling that they exist (wouldn't you?). It's hard to give individual attention in a lecture format, but you can at least communicate that you know they are there.

Then of course there are technologies you can use to communicate. These range from very low tech (the board) to medium tech (copied handouts, the overhead projector or film) to much more high tech (computer links to students at their desks). Keep in mind, as you consider what, if any, level of technology to use, that technology is a means to an end not an end in itself.[11] One of my colleagues in the department of instructional design, development, and evaluation (IDD&E) wears a button that says on top: "TECHNOLOGY IS THE AN-SWER!"; below that it says: "but what's the question?" If technology is to be of value it must be appropriate to the setting and the objective for which it is enlisted. Each technology has its relative strengths and weaknesses. For example, if you are telling a story with graphs, the board allows your students to see it unfold slowly, and it allows much of the information to be in front of them simultaneously (e.g., for development of a point). In contrast, an overhead projector allows you to face your students while you show them how things unfold, and it allows you to pre-draw particularly difficult graphs,[12] but it has limited space. For each technology there are tricks of the trade that you must keep in mind if it is going to be used effectively. For example, when using the board, it is generally a good idea to:
- Start at the top
- Write legibly and large enough to be seen (ask "can you see this?")
- Turn to talk, don't talk to the board
- Ask whether they have it before erasing
- Label clearly (e.g., graphs or charts)
- Use different colors to enhance clarity
- Separate different materials with dividing lines
- Erase previous material completely (reduces distractors)
- Put tedious stuff up before class or make it a handout.

Pacing a Lecture

This is an iterative process. Start at a pace that is comfortable for you, and see how it seems to feel for the students. Ask them. Do a

11. Innovation and technology are not an identity. Most of the most creative and effective innovations in classrooms are very low or no tech.

12. If the graphs are that difficult, you should probably also provide them in handout form.

quick survey at the end of the fifth day of class ("On a scratch piece of paper, tell me what you think about the pace of my lectures.") If most students score you "about right" with a few scoring "too fast" and some "too slow" then you are probably doing just fine. If the feedback is skewed one way or the other, decide whether there is a constructive adjustment you can (or need to) make.

Energizing Your Lecture

Ultimately, there will be no life in your lecture class if you don't bring it to the room. Your students want to be engaged, but they are depending on you to give them a reason to be. You must provide the catalyst that energizes the students and encourages them to invest in the endeavor. Such a catalyst can take many forms, but I think the most dependable is your own enthusiasm for the subject. That enthusiasm might be reflected in the joy the students see you feel for the beauty of the subject. It might be reflected in the fascination you display for the ways in which the subject can be applied to our day-to-day existence. Or it might come from a combination of these or from some other signal you send explicitly or implicitly which demonstrates that you really believe this stuff is worth the effort of learning. Whatever its source, some catalyst that energizes the room is necessary; without it, the life of the mind dies about five minutes into your lecture.

Be Yourself—A Real Person

Don't be a disembodied intellect. Allow the students to see that you are a human being with an imagination and fascination and concerns and visions and a sense of humor. Let down your wall of separation enough for them to relate to you as a person as well as a professor. Doing so makes communication easier because it breaks down some of the awe that some students have for the professor without in any way affecting the respect they should have for the position.

You Need Not Only Lecture in a Lecture

Obviously, you lecture in a lecture class, but you need not only lecture in a lecture. The smaller the class and the more flexible the room (e.g., do the chairs move? Is there a nearby space suitable for group activity?), the more you can do with nonlecture methods in what is a lecture course context. Choose the combination of tools that suits the needs of your students and your objectives for them.

Try Innovations—Don't Be Afraid to Make Mistakes

On this point I share a pearl of wisdom I received from Lew Hoffman, my supervising teacher when I was a student teacher preparing for secondary certification. After a particularly bad and depressing class day, I walked dejectedly into his room. I briefly described the debacle I had just left behind, and I speculated on other career options. His response was, "Evensky, remember the standard: you're doin' pretty good if you have more good days than bad days."

At the time that was not a particularly comforting remark. I thought, "What a dismal standard: 'more good days than bad days.' Can I really be happy in a career where it's a pretty good job when you do it well only a little more than half the time?" Well I persevered, and slowly but surely in the course of my career the Hoffman wisdom has become clearer to me. There are good reasons for bad days, and there are reasons for bad days that have nothing to do with you as the instructor. A reason for bad days that has nothing to do with you could be the rush parties the night before, or the chemistry exam that most of your class has in two hours, or news of a campus tragedy, or anything else that might impair or distract your students. The good reason for a bad day is an experiment in teaching that blows up in your face. If you don't experiment with your course content, your style, or both, you can't grow. A failed experiment costs a day; a successful experiment pays off for a lifetime. Take some chances, and grow.

Find Your Own Voice

The Best Style For Your Lecture

The best style for your lecture is the style that suits you best. In short, be yourself. When I first started teaching, at Hixson Junior High School, I team taught a class with a person who became a life-long friend, Tom Franey. I really admired the way Tom related to the kids, so in many ways I deferred to him in defining the culture of our classroom. When Tom moved on to another assignment, I was panic-stricken. I didn't have much confidence in myself, and I certainly didn't have a "style" of my own. So I tried to mimic the style of my good friend Tom. An aide who had worked with Tom and me together and now worked with me alone recognized my struggle. One day she sat me down and reflected on what she saw. She concluded with some words that have always meant a lot to me. She said, "Jerry, you aren't and never will be a very good Tom, but you can be a very good Jerry. Why don't you try being Jerry?" It took me a while to be comfortable with being just me, but I did find that I was much better as me than as Tom. Not only much better, but much happier.

I have colleagues who capture their classes with their humor, or their theatrics, or their booming voice. I have none of these assets. I'm not even sure how I would describe my own style. It's certainly pretty low-key. I just know it's mine, it's me, and most students seem to respond to it. Ultimately, that's all that matters.

Being Successful, Being Confident

Ultimately, your confidence will come from feeling that you are doing a good job. But where does it come from before you start? From preparing to do a good job. Good, careful preparation helps you move with self-assurance.

If you also ensure that your students are ready and if you keep yourself and them actively engaged in the process of the lecture, you are going to be OK. You'll learn to be ever more successful and with every success will come more confidence.

Learning to lecture is like learning anything else. First you have to understand, then you learn. I hope this piece has contributed something to your understanding. Understanding gives you the tools to learn, but the learning comes with practice, practice, practice.

Finally, and most important—do for yourself as you should for your students: Believe in yourself.

3

The Discussion/Recitation Section

KRISTI ANDERSEN AND KATALIN FABIAN

Many teaching assistants are responsible for conducting discussion sections which are part of a large lecture course, often at the introductory level.[1] Generally, these sections are relatively small (usually not more than twenty-five students) and meet once a week. These classes can be a critically important part of an undergraduate student's learning experience, since they allow time and attention for questions and the discussions which cannot take place during the large lecture. For students, the smaller sessions can provide a sense of community usually missing in large classes in a university setting. For the instructors who teach them, discussion sections can be a useful "middle level" of teaching experience, in between simply grading for and assisting a faculty member and teaching their own courses. Because the course syllabus and requirements typically are set by the faculty member or by the department, the discussion section instructor can concentrate on developing, within those already established frameworks, an atmosphere of fruitful and exciting interchange.

1. This chapter is a distillation of a handbook on discussion sections developed by the Syracuse University Political Science Department in meetings of discussion section leaders, introductory course faculty, and the graduate director, and in interviews with section leaders. The material appearing as extract (block quote) is taken from our interviews with our department's discussion section leaders during 1992–93. We thank Deb Kreidler of the Philosophy Department for making her departmental handout available to us. And we are grateful to the Political Science discussion section leaders who gave us their time for this collection of "common wisdom."

29

Some Things to Think About Before the Course Begins

Autonomy and course structure. What kinds of choices a discussion section leader can make about books, assignments, attendance, and topics of discussion depend strongly on the policies and practices of the department and the faculty member teaching the course. Sometimes discussion sections are seen as occasions for the ideas presented in the lectures to be repeated, reworked, and possibly elaborated. Other times, the discussion section leaders have more autonomy. They may have been involved in planning the course itself; they may have the opportunity to assign students additional tasks; they may be relatively free to structure the discussions in ways independent of the lectures. The important point here is that you should do everything you can to make sure you understand both the spoken and the unspoken rules about how much independence you have as an instructor. It is also important, whatever the structure of the course, that the students in your sections understand the relationship between the lecture and the sections. For example, is it expected that you will devote a great deal of time to reviewing the lecture? What is your relationship to the faculty member teaching the course? Are you responsible for grading the work of the students in your sections? Your department might or might not offer explicit orientation or training for its section leaders; in any case, you should not hesitate to ask questions of the professor and your peers until you have a good understanding of the overall course structure, expectations, and goals.

Regardless of course structure, the most successful courses are those with frequent, constructive communication between the professor teaching the course and the section leaders. Weekly meetings are one way to promote this; having the professor visit each section can also be helpful, both because it provides section leaders with good suggestions about how to improve their teaching style and because it communicates to students in the sections that the sections are important to both the professor and the section leader.

Classroom management. You probably can recall a class where even the first meeting whetted your appetite for the course material. The professor expressed a teaching philosophy that you appreciated, the expectations did not seem impossible, and you became interested in the other students in the class. Such is the ideal. But even if you are not fortunate enough to have an enthusiastic group of students, a good time slot for the section, or an accommodating room, you still can make the section very enjoyable and productive. Although you might not have complete autonomy in what material you present, you still have a huge influence on the success of the section, since you often know the students best and can adapt to their strengths and weaknesses.

Power issues are worth some thought in advance. You hold the power in your section: the students may very well perceive you as having much more authority than you think you have because you are responsible for a part of their grades and you are in charge of classroom behavior. Furthermore, students are rarely aware that the section leader may not be in control of what material is selected for the course. It's best, however, not to exploit your status. You need some authority but also quite a lot of flexibility and understanding. Try to rid your classroom of the "students against the teacher" image; your shared student status can forge a common platform.

Goal setting. Think about what you want to achieve in your class. Do you want to challenge the students' fundamental assumptions, or do you want to focus on expanding their lexical knowledge—or both? Being clear about your expectations for the class will help you to sort out which behavior you will appreciate and reward and which you will punish or just not tolerate. You may even want to think in advance about how you will respond to nuisances, such as students who read a newspaper or sleep through class, or students who are notoriously late for class or with assignments. If you announce your rules on the first day of class, nobody can say later that they were ignorant of your policies. In many introductory courses, you will be encouraged—sometimes required—to prepare a short (one-page) syllabus. Preparing and distributing the syllabus in itself expresses your authority, and it shows the students that you have particular expectations of them. You may want to include on it any crucial information pertinent to your handling of the class so that you can avoid later complaints and misunderstandings about expectations.

Another issue to consider is tone and style. Many topics in the social sciences and humanities are controversial; instructors often are comfortable with fairly adversarial talk, but undergraduates often are intimidated by an adversarial tone or perceive a matter of scientific argument as a personal attack on their beliefs. Sarcastic, pointed remarks—by you or the students—can turn the classroom into a hostile environment, where students will not feel comfortable expressing their thoughts. On the other hand, many teachers argue that by making strong challenges to students' arguments they prompt students' intellectual growth. Part of your decision about the tone you want to adopt obviously depends on your individual personality and how you relate to other people; it also will depend on the topics you are covering. Whatever style of interaction you adopt (and it is important to note that each instructor eventually finds his or her own particular style), try to use silence to your advantage. If you ask a question, *wait* for a response; students are likely to be much more uncomfortable with the silence than you are, once you get used to it.

The first class meeting. The first day of class is important in establishing a positive atmosphere, as well as conveying your expectations to the students. Writing your name, office and phone numbers on the board the first day, as well as telling the students something about your own background, are classic—and useful—ways to begin. During the first section meeting, discuss the mechanics of the course, and what you expect from the students. You might find it very useful to declare during the first class meeting that a discussion section is not the same thing as a review section; such a misapprehension is further reduced if the professor teaching the course reconfirms the idea of independent discussion sections. There are several useful ways to get acquainted in class. Instead of using the class roster, for example, you might distribute cards for students to fill out with their name, major, special interests or related courses, and what they expect to learn from the course. You can then use these cards to take attendance each time and better associate names with real people. Or you could divide the entering class by assigning numbers randomly twice. Each student has to find the other student with their number, and after a few minutes of discussion, the pairs introduce each other. Or you could require students to set up an appointment with you during your office hours in the first couple of weeks of class, and simply meet and talk individually.

Another important beginning activity is making contact with students with learning or other disabilities, by announcing that anyone who has need for test-taking, note-taking, or other accommodation should feel free to come and discuss it with you. Then be prepared to follow the policies of your department or institution regarding any accommodation. Be aware that if during the course of the term you observe a severe discrepancy between a student's class participation and his or her written work, a learning disability may be the problem.

Encouraging Active Engagement with the Material

The discussion section ideal is a lively, informed, conversation that furthers everyone's understanding of the course material. Because discussion sections are just that—aimed at producing discussion—and because they are much smaller than the typical lower- or middle-level undergraduate class, achieving that ideal is really within your grasp. Aim, then, for active learning, which in this context you can take to mean learning in which students are *not* passively taking notes simply to protect themselves when the exam comes; students are not just listening but are hearing what you and their peers are saying; they are making connections and are eager to make others aware of these connections; they are taking in the material of the course and thinking about how that material relates to other courses, books they've read, their personal problems, or an article in the *New York Times*.

Weekly writing assignments. How can you create this level of active, conscious engagement? To begin with, it sometimes might help to require students to do something in writing each week. You might try to stimulate students by asking them to turn in at the beginning of each session questions they have about the readings or lectures. This method can substitute for taking attendance, and it exerts a continuous pressure on students to keep up with the assigned material. It also allows you to use students' own questions as a basis for the discussion, which helps pull them into the conversation.

Role playing and other activities. Beyond meeting minimal requirements such as written questions, students ideally should get involved with, and think deeply and critically about, the topics covered in discussion. This is not easy when you consider that over the course of a semester you may be discussing a range of topics at varying levels of abstraction, and be confronted with students with varying individual learning styles. Thus, it will be useful to think about how you can vary the format of your section to take account of all the points you want to make and to provide a variety of different learning experiences for your students. Some discussion section instructors use role-playing exercises, in which students take on the roles of particular actors in the American or international political systems, for example. For the most part, such exercises are successful in getting students to talk and think about important issues.

I provided an article on health care reform, which they read quickly in the beginning of the class; then I asked for volunteers for different roles, such as the representatives of the drug industry, doctors' association, and people without insurance. Then we selected three senators who, after hearing the different groups and consulting with each other, made a decision concerning which reform package they would adopt. Then the whole class questioned and analyzed what led them to decide in this manner. This was the best class meeting during the semester; I wish I had more classes like that!

I held mock presidential debates in my sections. The debates were divided on the basis of issue areas: economy, foreign policy, and health care. The students gave me their top three choices, indicating which issue and candidate they wanted to represent. As it turned out, each debate had about four students representing each candidate, who then took turns in answering the questions directed at them by the rest of the class. The candidates were also expected to submit a one-page paper discussing why they supported their position, while the others wrote on why the issue was important. Judging by the debate papers I received, I think everyone learned a lot about the 1992 campaign.

In many areas there are computer simulations or other media available for student use. Using videos, slides, or an occasional guest lecturer may also help to break up the format of the class and provide insights from a different point of view. Discussion sections on topics such as international relations or American politics obviously lend themselves to the strategy of tying the lecture and reading material to current events, but classes in other disciplines might use the technique as well, drawing on recently published works, reviews, or newspaper articles.

Using tools. Such seemingly trivial habits as providing handouts or using the blackboard or overhead projector can aid and reinforce student learning by helping you to outline, clarify major points, or present data or diagrams. Be sure that, when you use the blackboard, talk not to it but to the students, and make sure that you are comfortable with the overhead projector before you use it.

Student dynamics. Active learning is much more likely to occur in a situation of mutual respect between instructor and students. Listen to your students and take their ideas seriously; in fact, you may want to keep track of good ideas as they occur by putting them on the blackboard, or eventually in a notebook so you later can retrieve and use them. Give space to students who are struggling to articulate ideas that are not yet clear to them. Try to remember back to your own problems with the material: it will make you more understanding of your students' problems.

Finally, be realistic; if not all your students are attentive and enthusiastic, it does not mean that you are an inept teacher. A technique or an example that does not work in one case might work in another —and vice versa! Remain flexible, and try something else!

Challenges and Opportunities

Perhaps the first challenge to any instructor teaching a new class is learning the names of the students. Over and over, students say that their positive feelings about a class increase when the instructor seems to know them. When you address students by name, it also lets them get to know one another and helps move the class toward the goal of having conversations where everyone talks with everyone else. For these reasons, learning everyone's name as soon as possible is a worthwhile goal.

Problems (or challenges) will inevitably occur. Sometimes particular students will be disruptive or won't let anyone else get a word in edgewise. You will have to work out your own solutions to such problems—but taking the student aside after class and stressing your desire for wider participation may help. Another common problem is the student who simply does not care, who has calculated the minimum that needs to be done to get an acceptable grade and refuses to do more.

> Although I always took attendance, merely showing up was not enough to get the full 15 percent of the course grade which was assigned to the discussion section. For a while students did submit two questions for each class, but this just did not work out. Good students who read the material submitted the questions, but for students who could not care less, preparing questions was a totally senseless assignment. So I modified the requirement: those who wanted, could continue this practice, and it raised their grade.

> The biggest challenge was to get the students to show up and prepare for the discussion section. At first I took attendance, but that wasn't totally successful. Then we started giving random quizzes based on the readings, which worked better than taking attendance.

Another challenge will be students—particularly, but not only, first year students—who are afraid to ask questions or to put themselves out on an intellectual limb by making new or different arguments. Your goal is to make the environment comfortable enough for students to ask questions or make suggestions. On the other hand, you need to keep a balance between the sometimes tangential material students feel comfortable suggesting and the material you feel you need to present or review.

Evaluating Your Performance. It's only natural to want to know how you are doing. One easy way to find out is to ask your students. After a week or two you might ask them to respond anonymously to questions such as: Are my directions clear? Can you hear me? Do I explain points enough or in too much detail? Do you feel free to ask me questions? Sometimes your department will conduct its own evaluation, for example, informal evaluations distributed about half-way through the semester and seen only by the section leader and by the faculty member teaching the course. Early evaluations like these can help you think about how to change or improve the class format in time to have an impact.

Other ways to get feedback are to have another section leader or the professor teaching the course observe your performance in class. Finally, many departments encourage videotaping of discussions. Sitting down with a fellow instructor to watch and critique the video can be an extremely enlightening and positive experience.

Discussion sections add an important element to your students' educational experience. They will especially appreciate the small classes, the access to you as a source of information and feedback, and the sense of community they gain. Moreover, faculty teaching courses with discussion sections appreciate the added dimension the sections contribute to their lectures. Your role as discussion section leader is a responsibility to be taken seriously—but one that can be both satisfying and educational.

4

The Studio

BARBARA WALTER AND JANE HENDLER

In a studio course, the processes of learning and creating are as important as the product. Often students work on their assignments during class time. Both these processes and the product are discussed. Learning evolves over time in successive cycles of action and reflection. Students might rework an assignment several times, so they learn and practice techniques and skills during class and on their own. Through discussions and critiques students learn how to talk about and evaluate their work.

The Learning Environment

The studio classroom is not a static space. The space must have the potential for interaction and the flexibility to maximize participation and communication. Once you have received your classroom assignment, visit the room so that you can become familiar with its environment. Feeling comfortable in the classroom can help build your confidence. Talk to someone who has taught in that room; ask about any idiosyncrasies. Does the marching band practice at the same time in the room above? Can the room accommodate your special need, such as audiovisual equipment, moveable furniture, or window shades? Will its size accommodate the number of students enrolled? Are there enough seats? Also try the acoustics. Will you have to speak loudly to be heard in the back? Try to check the room early enough so that changes can be made; if the room cannot be changed, at least you will have time to request shades or more seats.

If the classroom will not always meet the needs of the class, perhaps you can find a room that will, such as a slide projection room, computer cluster, or seminar room, and reserve it for those occasions. Decide what your multimedia needs are, so you can reserve projectors, videotape monitors, and the like. Is there enough chalkboard space, or will you need an overhead projector?

Start a list of contact people and their phone numbers. Besides listing the phone numbers of the secretary of the department, also list faculty advisor, faculty mentor, and peers. Find out who to contact if there is a problem with the classroom or if you need to leave a note for your class. Record the phone numbers of Physical Plant and Audio Visual Services. Include the phone numbers for Security and Safety on your list.

Course Preparation

Review any teaching material given to you. What are the goals of the curriculum? Do you understand them? Present these goals in objectives and requirements, and express them clearly in your syllabus. If students have paid materials fees, also list what those fees cover. Once you have organized the semester in the syllabus, decide what supplies, materials, and texts are required. First find out what is available without having to be ordered. Which supplies and materials are your responsibility to provide and which are the responsibility of the students? Find out whom you need to contact, how to do the ordering, and if there are deadlines. In addition to the more concrete objectives presented in your syllabus give some thought to the goals you might set in addition to those outlined in the curriculum. Some of these goals may deal with behavior and attitude. For example, part of your teaching philosophy may be to help the students become independent thinkers with mutual respect for one another. Begin to form a strategy for moving toward these goals and any the students themselves might have. Consider what brings them to a university? What do you assume they want from the course and from you? Some may want job training, a good grade, or to make their parents happy. You may want them to learn specific information, values, or social presentation. These assumptions may have an impact on how you teach and what you teach.

Projects and Assignments

When giving assignments, be sure that the objectives are clear. State the requirements, limitations, and variables. Give the students a time frame and a due date. Do you need to stress process, closure, or both? How will the assignment be evaluated? Once the assignment has been presented, allow time for clarification. The presentation of the assignment may also be a valuable part of the learning experience. There will be times when students will ask questions about routine matters such as due dates or course requirements. Sometimes it may be more appropriate, however, to answer questions with questions, when you want the student to make connections through self-discovery. Ask a question that will lead the student toward the answer. Having the student answer the question may help give that person confidence. You may ask the student to clarify what the question really is. Pay attention to the questions asked. They will help you gauge the rate of learning and where areas of confusion exist. A studio course typically includes some work days, that is, days when the students work on their assignments during class. Before the work day, establish guidelines for how the time will be used. Emphasize that the students need to attend class. What process they use in completing the assignment is as important as the product. For you to evaluate that process, you must be present to witness it, because most creative processes are not documented as experiments in a lab notebook, for example. It is advantageous for both you and the students to be able to talk about the process during the experience, rather than after the fact. Also, tell the students what preparations they need to make for the work day. Do they need special supplies? Do they need to bring research to class? Follow through; don't treat this as a time when you do not have to teach. All that is changing is the method of teaching.

Critiquing the Assignment

On the due day of the assignment, review the objectives and other criteria with the class. What were the immediate goals of the assignment? Follow the guidelines that were set when the assignment was given. Although there are many ways of assessing an assignment, critiquing is a particularly useful method. Before you bring your students together for a critiquing session, share with them the general goals of the critique and the specific requirements and guidelines that they should focus on for each project. A distinguishing feature of studio classrooms is the practice of peer reviewing or critiquing. Collaborating with peers to critique assignments maximizes student learning in a studio environment in several ways. First, students begin to develop a self-reflective response to their own work. Second, they receive constructive feedback that will help them redirect or revise their approach to their project so they can continue with the next steps toward completion. Further, peer critiquing can strengthen the skill of critical judgment in that students will learn to make informed responses to a variety of aesthetic approaches. Finally, the emphasis on learning as a *process* and not merely as a product is enhanced as students begin to recognize learning as successive cycles of action and reflection.

In addition, peer critiquing contributes to the affective aspects of learning. As students begin to understand their roles and responsibilities in critiquing, they likely will become more self-confident, more independent, and more open-minded in their responses and attitudes toward inquiry. A benefit can be better group dynamics and mutual respect and support among students.

Effective peer critiquing requires planning and modeling on your part. First-year students, in particular, may find the idea of publicly sharing their projects or their writing intimidating or confusing. A little forethought on your part will help you avoid sessions that become unproductive or frustrating.

When to critique. A good time to critique is at the end of their first major project. At this stage, students can reflect on the project as a whole and consider alternatives and future directions. However, you sometimes will want to critique at an intermediary stage, so that students' peers and you can give some direction for further revision and reshaping to be completed before students submit a finished assignment. At midterm and finals are other times to consider critiquing; these are good points at which to consider an instructor-student conference, so that you can give individual attention to a student's work. Students should know ahead of time if an assignment will be critiqued and what the topic of the critique will be.

What type of critique to use. Critiques can be structured in a variety of ways: large-group sessions, small groups, one-on-one formats, and either oral or written feedback. Each type has both advantages and disadvantages, depending on the type of project to be critiqued, how familiar students are with critiquing, classroom dynamics, and the time available. Large-group critiques (involving the entire class) can be especially useful if you want to model the process itself. The particular advantages of large-group sessions are that many viewpoints can be expressed and you can facilitate discussion more readily. However, large-group sessions take longer, so time considerations may require you to use small groups instead; critiquing twenty students' projects takes much less time if students work in groups of three or four, as opposed to doing twenty critiques in a large group. Another disadvantage is that some students will be less assertive and less at ease speaking in large groups.

In addition to encouraging quieter students to participate and managing classroom time more efficiently, small-group sessions have the advantage of being more intimate, in that students oftentimes respond more candidly to one another's work. Be aware that small groups function less effectively if the members are friends or if they all tend to be quiet. Appointing a group leader to facilitate, or working out good "mixes" of students, will help avoid such problems.

Another method—using student pairs for one-on-one sessions— is effective for students who would benefit from having just one other student act as sounding board, observer, and listener in helping them solve a troublesome problem or approach. Student pairs can reduce the anxiety of large-group sessions and allow students to concentrate on just one other project. A disadvantage is that students receive only one point of view. One-on-one critiques between the student and you have the advantage of giving both of you a better sense of how the student is understanding the project.

Whether you decide to use oral or written critiques or a combination of both will depend on the time constraints, whether the critiques are intended to be formal or informal, whether you think students will benefit from having a record of the discussion, and whether making critiques written could help students to articulate the cognitive processes and their personal reactions.

Participation guidelines. Fostering an atmosphere of mutual support, trust, and respect is key to a productive critique, but it requires some ground rules and guidelines for participation. Make students aware of these rules prior to the session. Some guidelines to consider are the following: everyone should be expected to participate; both strengths and weaknesses of the assignment should be discussed; comments should never be personal but instead directed at the work; disagreements will develop and some comments will be subjective, but critiques are discussions, not evaluations. When you are modeling a large-group critique for students who are unfamiliar with the process, or when you are facilitating a large-group session, try to keep the critique focused and relatively short. Avoid letting the critique continue for so long a time that students become bored and restless. If the class becomes too divided over an issue or a situation of class-versus-instructor develops, try to refocus the discussion by asking questions. Or end the discussion temporarily, and state that you will return to it later but that the class needs to move on.

As your students and you become more proficient at critiquing, you should find that questions become the primary mode of interaction. Ask more questions than you make statements. Begin the critique with comments or questions from someone other than the student whose project is under consideration—this strategy helps avoid the situation where the student merely defends or excuses everything before anyone else contributes. The strategy is especially useful if your students are inexperienced or insecure. The following questions will help launch your discussion:

- Does the assignment solve the problem or give convincing alternatives?
- What do you think the student was trying to do? Your impressions?
- Is there anything you would change? Weaknesses?
- What would you keep? Strengths?
- What questions does the student have who did the work?
- What did the student intend? How close did he or she come to what the audience picked up?

Summarizing the objectives. A summary and self-evaluation are important components of critiques. You can prompt a brief summary at the end of each student's critique by asking the student what she or he thinks are the particular strengths and weaknesses of the project and how it might be revised. Solicit responses from the student about the assignment—where did he or she have difficulties and what worked successfully? In addition, it might be beneficial for you to solicit a critique of the assignment itself from the entire class. Ask students to try to relate the current project to future assignments and goals. This will help them recognize that the particular processes, skills, and knowledge they applied on the current project are a foundation upon which to base their next level of learning.

Individual Portfolios

You might find it helpful to require that each student keep an individual portfolio that will serve as a collection site for his or her past as well as current projects. Portfolios can be used to organize everything a student has worked on to date—including unfinished drafts and notes on future projects, as well as formal presentations.

Another way to compile a portfolio is to have students select their most representative work—works to date, best efforts, or works-in-progress. A portfolio also can be used for course evaluation purposes. A particular advantage of a studio portfolio is that it is a portable record of work that students can carry outside the university setting to job interviews or visits to prospective graduate schools.

Resolving Conflicts in the Studio

In a studio course, teaching the individual student as well as the group takes on new meaning. In contrast to the large lecture situation, the individual student can be seen, his or her name and face recognized by the instructor, and oftentimes is more willing to speak out. There is more opportunity for personal involvement, for both the student and the instructor. Compliments, conflicts, and complaints also might be more obvious. The compliments are easy to deal with; the conflicts and complaints are more difficult to resolve.

If a conflict arises between a student and you or between classmates, try to establish the history of the conflict. Is it a simple misunderstanding or miscommunication? Is it a difference of opinion? Has it been building over time, or has it just started? A conflict or complaint is much easier to resolve when it is small. What is your point of view as the instructor? What is the point of view of the student? If you feel that you cannot easily resolve the situation, get some help. Work toward the best outcome for all involved.

Grading

Grading in many studio courses is less objective, in fact, than in courses where grades are based on written tests. In a studio course, the grades given typically are based on a variety of criteria. Since the creative process itself is also important in many studios, the product is not the only variable. What progress the student makes from the beginning to the end of the semester might be important; work ethic, attitude, effort, and risk taking also might be factors. Include your criteria for grading in the syllabus, then stick to them. Clearly state your objective and subjective standards. Remember that the same criteria should apply to everyone in the class; you cannot change them from individual to individual.

5

The Laboratory

TRACY MANNARA, SALMA ABU AYYASH, MARY CANNELLA,
CHARLES WIDENER, AND FREDERICK PHELPS

As a TA, you might be asked to instruct in a laboratory. The following will give you guidelines to assist you in performing your duties as a lab instructor.

Preparation

Meet with the supervising professor in charge as soon as you get your assignment. You need to get a tour of the lab and learn the lab procedures, including who gives the equipment to the students, where the supplies are, and where dangers such as high voltage electricity and corrosive chemicals are. You want to be clear about what is expected of you in the laboratory: Do you give a lecture; if so, what material should be covered? Who will make up the quizzes and exams, and who will grade them? How are final grades determined and how much say will you have in those final grades? If other sections of the same lab are being taught by other TAs, you will want to be introduced to them; set up a weekly meeting for all TAs and the professor in charge. Make sure you know what special items the students must bring to the first lab, such as lab notebooks, textbooks, or any special equipment, so that you can ensure that they are prepared. It is best to do all of these things before the semester begins.

Perform labs before the actual lab session. In most laboratories, students will purchase or be given a procedure to follow, which will take them step-by-step through each lab. You should perform each lab experiment or project yourself before the students do it. In this way, you will be familiar with the equipment to be used and the results to

44

be expected. If other TAs are teaching sections whose activities coincide with yours, you might set up a time for all of you to practice the lab together.

Study the theories being covered in order to be prepared to answer students' questions. The purpose of most laboratories is for students to observe in practice the theories they have been taught in lectures. Laboratories not only teach good methods; they also provide evidence for theories and confirm hypotheses. Therefore, you must be aware of the underlying theories, hypotheses, and so on that are being tested, and, in turn, make the students aware of them.

Know why specific equipment is to be used and how to use it. In some instances, the students will need special equipment to perform an experiment. You should be aware of not only how to use the special equipment but also why it is used.

If applicable, research the relevance of the experiment to real life. Making a lab more meaningful in this way will motivate the students to learn what is really going on. No one wants to spend hours working on something that seems irrelevant. Sometimes the students might be allowed to propose an experiment of their own that they would like to perform; before agreeing, you or the professor in charge will need to verify that the proposed experiment in fact reinforces the theories being applied in the lab. In addition, you might want to suggest new experiments that would also enhance the students' learning of the lab theory; again the professor in charge will need to verify the applicability.

Make the objectives of each experiment clear. Each lab has certain objectives; i.e., what the students are to learn by doing the lab. These objectives are not a secret. Tell the students what they are expected to find, and leave finding it as the challenge. In this way students will be rewarded for their hard work when they get the expected results.

Anticipate problems. Problems are bound to arise. When you are practicing the lab ahead of time, try to explore different scenarios in which a student might make a mistake, and anticipate what effect the mistake would have on the outcome of the experiment. Brainstorm with the other TAs or the professor to think of anything else that could go wrong with the experiment, and how you are going to correct it. One of the hardest things about teaching a laboratory is determining how to fix a problem the student is having with his or her experiment. Knowing how to handle problems comes partly with experience, but preparation can help. Even with good preparation, there will be times when you simply cannot determine what is wrong.

If no other help is available, inform the student that you will try to solve the problem before the next lab meeting. It is all right not to know everything; but that's no excuse for coming to lab unprepared.

Keep in touch with the professor in charge. Your professor has witnessed these experiments many times; try to meet regularly and do not hesitate to ask questions about what he or she expects from the experiments or what problems the students usually face, and the like.

Atmosphere

Make an orderly beginning. The lab atmosphere is typically less orderly than a classroom setting; therefore, an organized and orderly beginning is essential. At the beginning of each lab session, present any theory that needs to be discussed or explain the experiment, making clear its objectives. Starting the session in this way will assure that each student arrives at the appointed lab time. The beginning of the session is also the time to explain rules and to exert some authority; you are in charge, and the students should be expected to do what you tell them to do. Later you can wander around the lab and help each student more informally.

Maintain a comfortable, yet professional relationship with your students. How you act in lab depends partially on your personality. If you feel more comfortable staying at the front of the room and maintaining a more formal relationship with your students, that is your choice, as long as you continue to help them with their problems. On the other hand, if you prefer to wander around the room and interact with them more informally, that is also acceptable. However, if you tend toward being informal, what you must keep in mind is that you will be giving these students a grade. For that reason, being their "buddy" and socializing with them is risky.

Check your university's policy regarding teacher/student socializing. You do not want to put yourself in a situation where you cannot be objective in your grading.

Be attuned to laboratory cultures. Even though the labs have an atmosphere much different from regular classroom sessions, you are still the instructor, and you should be aware of the different classroom cultures that you might help in creating. An open classroom culture is usually learner-centered and content-oriented; the instructor acts as a facilitator, and the learners are activists. In such a culture, multiple assessment instruments typically are used. In addition, personal and cultural considerations are relevant to teaching and learning.

This is the preferred method for laboratory instruction. In contrast, a closed classroom culture is instructor-centered and coverage-oriented; the instructor is in command, and the learners are passive recipients. In a closed classroom examinations usually are the only assessment instrument used. Personal and cultural considerations are peripheral to teaching and learning.

Policy

Grading—choose your evaluation methods carefully. Which methods you use for grading is a very important issue. Do you test students on the theory or the application of the theory (methodology)? Do you consider the theory fundamental and assume the students learned it in another setting? Is the theory new and being taught in the lab, so that testing on theory is necessary? Do you want to test both theory and methodology equivalently? You need to answer these questions and choose your evaluation methods appropriately. If your emphasis is on methodology, you might want to base most of the lab grade on weekly lab notebook entries and a number of practical exams. If your emphasis is on theory, quizzes and exams might be sufficient. In either case, you must decide and convey your emphasis and evaluation methods to the students at the beginning of the term, and you should not change them later.

Attendance—emphasize its importance. Laboratory is a "hands-on" experience. Attendance is mandatory. Students must be made aware of this, and you must strictly apply specific penalties in cases of unexcused absences.

Integrity—hold out high expectations. In most laboratories, students will work with partners. But that should not mean that one student does all the work. Each student must do his or her own work when preparing for labs and in writing up lab reports. A more informal environment does not mean lax attention to issues of individual responsibility such as cheating, copying, faking results, and the like.

Work in groups—help students contribute fully. Most lab situations involve students working with one or more partners. Oftentimes, tasks are not shared evenly, and one or more of the partners will not learn the techniques that are the objectives in the lab. Strongly encourage the students to take turns when working in a group, and stress that each student must know how to complete each part of the experiment. This is especially important if the students' proficiency in the lab will be tested by individual practical exams. Sometimes in a team situation, personality conflicts may arise; in extreme cases, lab partners cannot get along well enough to work together. If all attempts to overcome differences have failed, you should split up such partners. Students' opportunity to learn should not be adversely affected because they cannot get along with their lab partners.

Safety

Allow no food or drinks in the lab. This is a good general rule. No matter what discipline you are working in, the lab is not the cafeteria. Allowing eating and drinking in the lab promotes a setting that not only is too informal but also is dangerous.

Be aware of your legal liability. Suits have been filed on occasion against science instructors. Practicing safety in the lab—by systematically assessing the risks of injury and controlling them—is probably the best way to reduce your chances of being found negligent.

Insist on adherence to laboratory safety guidelines. Each lab should have printed material available that explains all the safety procedures and requirements. Make sure you and your students thoroughly understand them; you probably should spend part of your first lab session discussing that information. Frequently remind your students of those safety guidelines. Set a good example for your students by always practicing the proper safety measures and following the guidelines yourself while demonstrating any experiments. Always stress the correct usage of supplies and equipment. Encourage students to develop a responsible concern for safety.

Be familiar with emergency equipment. You and all your students must know the location of any necessary safety equipment, such as circuit breakers, fire extinguishers, first aid kits, eye-wash facilities, and fire blankets.

Plan for emergencies. Early on determine which of your students or other personnel available can be called upon to perform emergency procedures such as CPR.

Anticipate hazards. When you are practicing the experiments ahead of time, have safety in mind; look for potential dangers. In your introduction to the students discuss thoroughly the safety procedures associated with each experiment because the procedures might not be clear in the general guidelines. Make sure students have absorbed these safety instructions before the experiments begin.

Check for safety signs and emergency instructions. Safety signs should be clear and should identify the location of any emergency equipment. Point them out to your students. Also encourage your students to read the posted emergency instructions and to know where they can locate emergency telephone numbers and the nearest telephone.

Make a student safety contract. Have your students read, understand, and sign a student safety contract, in which they declare their willingness to follow all safety instructions: to protect their eyes, hands, face, and body while performing experiments; to know where to get help fast; to know the location of the first aid and safety equipment, and how to use it; and to conduct themselves in a safe and responsible manner in the laboratory at all times.

File accident reports. Report accidents or hazardous incidents immediately. Have them evaluated by the departmental safety committee. Also discuss these occurrences and their causes with the students.

Prohibit use of labs during nonlab hours. Prohibit students from performing any experiments when they are alone in the lab. Insist that a lab attendant be available. Identify certain hazardous experiments that should be performed only in your presence, and make these hazardous situations clear.

Be alert! Participate in the labs as much as possible. Walk and look around and supervise the experiments. Ask your students questions, point out mistakes, and encourage better and safer procedures.

By following these guidelines for promoting good laboratory preparation, atmosphere, policy, and safety, you will enjoy a successful term as a lab TA.

6

Office Hours and Tutoring

LAWRENCE J. LARDY AND MARY K. PORTER

Office hours are important for both instructor and student. This is a time (and there are few such opportunities) for you to get to know your students as individuals and for students to see you as a person as well as their instructor. Office hours provide an occasion for you to observe in detail how well the course material is understood and to discover where students are having problems. At the same time, they give students an opportunity to meet you singly or in small groups and to ask questions they might be reluctant to ask in class.

Scheduling Office Hours

Most departments require instructors to hold several office hours each week. At the beginning of the semester, choose at least three hours per week (or more, if recommended by your department) during which you will be available to see students. Of course, to increase the likelihood that each student will be free to attend, it is best to schedule office hours at a variety of times and days.

Announce your schedule of office hours in the first class meeting and include it as part of the written course syllabus you distribute at the beginning of the semester. Throughout the course, especially if it is evident some students are falling behind, continue to announce your schedule and encourage students to take advantage of this extra time that you are available to help them. Invite students who cannot attend the scheduled office hours to make an appointment at another time. Make it clear that you are accessible and that they should feel free to ask questions on the course material, course prerequisites, or other issues connected with the course. After you have scheduled and

announced your office hours, be absolutely certain you keep them
and that you are there for the full, scheduled period. If you must
cancel an office hour, announce this in class beforehand, if possible,
and post a note on your office door restating the cancellation.

Office Hour Sessions

When working with students individually, it is extremely useful
to have a sense of the source of their difficulty. Thus, a little time
spent identifying a problem is usually worthwhile, but keep in mind
that an accurate and complete diagnosis is difficult to make, especially
in a few minutes. When exploring why a student might be having a
problem, don't grill the student—be careful not to make the student
feel you are administering an oral exam! Review the principles already covered in the class, and get a sense of how well the student has
mastered them. If the student's responses indicate that prerequisite
knowledge is missing, try to get the student to recall it. If the student
seems unclear about some of the course material, offer a variety of
alternative explanations from different points of view.

You are not expected to reteach class lessons for individual students during these office hour sessions, especially for students who
were absent without excuse. Besides, students who were in class and
have come to you for further help probably will not benefit from a
repeat of the same presentation. Instead, try to determine why the
students have not caught on to material presented in the classroom.
Remember: most learning is the result of student effort, not yours,
and without that effort you cannot help them as expected.

When a student comes for help on a homework assignment that
would take you just minutes to do yourself, avoid the temptation to
show him or her your clever solution. Rather, try to draw out the
approach you have in mind. Be patient, ask leading questions, and
offer encouragement when he or she is on the right track. When you
suspect faulty study habits are the root of the difficulty, ask the student how he or she studies the material and what attempts he or she
has made on the homework assignments. Ask for the student's own
assessment of his or her methods of study. When needed, make clear
and definite suggestions on how those study habits might be im-
proved. This also would be an opportunity to mention any other
departmental or institutional services that are available that might
help the student.

Take advantage of these opportunities to discuss the course with students. Try to ascertain how they feel about you and the course; use any information you gather about their progress to assess the pace of the course and to identify misconceptions and problems that might be common to students in the class. Often you can use the information you gain in talking to individual students to guide your teaching of the class as a whole. Consider addressing in a future class meeting problems and issues mentioned by several students during office hours. The students are likely to appreciate your being in touch with their concerns and with the problems they are experiencing with the course.

Advising

Often students will come to your office for advice of one kind or another. Always be a sympathetic listener. However, restrict your recommendations to areas where you are knowledgeable; in all other cases, refer students to an appropriate office or other instructor. Frequently, students will ask whether they can still pass the course, or what score they need on the final exam to get a certain final grade. In such situations, it is best not to make any promises about future grades. Normally, it is sufficient to simply review the grading policies for the course, which should be printed on the course syllabus, and to remind students of their record to date. Of course, even in cases where that record is dismal and there is little hope of success in the course, you should treat such students with respect and as adults.

Students also commonly ask for advice on whether they should drop the course. It is important here to keep in mind that dropping a course can have nonacademic implications, such as an impact on a student's financial aid status. Thus, students contemplating such a move should first consult their academic advisor, or an advisor in their home college.

Tutoring

You also will interact with students individually in cases in which you have agreed to act as a tutor. As a tutor, your position is somewhat different from that of the course instructor, and with that different position come different responsibilities. Under no circumstances should you accept any money for tutoring a student enrolled in a course that you are currently teaching. As a tutor, be sure to discuss your hourly fee before the tutoring sessions begin to avoid a misunderstanding about this issue; you might want to ask other tutors in your department what they charge in order to determine an appropriate fee.

If you make an appointment to tutor a student, make sure to keep the appointment and arrive promptly at the agreed-upon meeting place. Ask before the tutoring session what material the student would like to cover in the session, decide what you will need to prepare for the session, and do the necessary preparation work before meeting. If you come to a tutoring session unprepared, you are likely to waste the student's time and will appear unprofessional.

If during a tutoring session the student asks you questions about homework or assignments given in class, answer carefully; it is best to check with the student's instructor before you help the student with any work that is to be handed in. Even if the work is not to be handed in, don't simply do the work yourself; instead, encourage the student to do the work as you watch and give the necessary guidance. Above all, avoid making negative comments about the student's instructor or that instructor's grading policy.

Sensitivity Issues

Whether you are interacting with students on an individual basis or with the class as a whole, recognize and be sensitive to the diversity of your students. Pay attention to the language you use and the examples you give. Use language that is nonsexist. Do not make derogatory jokes or offensive remarks about ethnicity, sexual orientation, or other areas of diversity. Try to use examples that recognize diversity, and ones that challenge stereotypes.

Be sensitive to the individual and cultural differences of your students, and be conscious of the stereotypes you may have learned in the past. Get to know your students as individuals. Have high expectations for all of your students, regardless of their gender, ethnicity, and ability or disability, and treat each student with respect.

To face charges of sexual harassment is extremely unpleasant. Learn your institution's policies and guidelines about the kinds of behaviors that are inappropriate. Being prepared and aware will go a long way toward helping you avoid having to deal with charges of this kind. It is a good idea to leave your office door open during office hours; this practice will be welcomed by students and will help convey that the meeting will be on a strictly professional basis.

Summary

To get the most out of your office hours, keep the following in mind. Student visits during office hours offer opportunities to assess the learning progress of visiting students and, by extrapolation, of the entire class. Schedule office hours at a variety of times to encourage students to take advantage of them. Always be present during scheduled office hours and if changes are necessary announce them in advance during class. Be patient, sympathetic, and supportive as you help students understand and use the ideas studied in the course.

PART TWO

Enhancing Learning and Teaching

7

Assessment of Student Work

MICHAEL FLUSCHE

For generations, we college teachers have been cloned by the same process. When we emerge from our graduate studies, newly minted degrees in hand, and take our first full-time teaching position —or when, as graduate students, we take on our first teaching assistantship—we all tend to do the same thing: we teach as we were taught. That is, we model our teaching style, techniques, and content on the one or two teachers who made the greatest impression on us. And this is good. Most of us have been blessed with an instructor or two who truly deserves to be imitated, and the art of good teaching deserves to be passed from generation to generation. The limitation is that many of the models of good teaching that appeal to the academically inclined—those of us who go on to graduate school—may not be the most effective for the vast majority of students, especially for those who struggle in the classroom. Also, the models we remember most clearly may well be the most recent ones, from our advanced or graduate-level courses.

Great Teachers

There are probably three types or models of great teachers that we remember although, of course, none of these three types exists in a pure state in reality. First, we all remember at least one great lecturer, an articulate scholar whose dazzling performance was a tour de force of intellectual pyrotechnics or whose vivid anecdotes made the material come alive. Some of these master teachers are legendary and are occasionally written up in the *New Yorker* or similar magazines. Others, in a low-keyed and self-effacing manner, covered the course material in an efficient, clear, and logical fashion. We look back and marvel at how much organic chemistry, macroeconomics, or calculus we learned each class as they relentlessly pressed on. And then we recall the teachers who put students first, who defined their task not as teaching physics, journalism, or marketing, but rather as helping students learn physics, journalism, or marketing. These are the teachers who on occasion may have spent as much time writing letters of recommendation for students as they did in preparing for class.

Classroom Assessment

All of these great teachers probably shared a common practice. They read the faces of their students and noted their body language; they were genuinely concerned when their students did poorly on tests and exams; and from year to year they adapted their courses in light of what seemed to work. That is, they practiced a type of informal, intuitive, part-time classroom assessment.

The good news is that we can, in this respect, be better even than our model teachers. For today's students, classroom assessment techniques give us extremely powerful and flexible tools that open up a new level and style of communication from instructor to student and from student to instructor. They build upon all the lessons that master teachers have been handing down for generations, and they take into account the things that students tell us about what makes effective teaching.[1]

What, then, is this thing called classroom assessment? Simply put, it is a series of techniques that help instructors do systematically and thoroughly what good teachers have always tried to do: find out what students are actually learning in the classroom and how well they are learning it. It also subtly shifts the way we think about teaching by taking the spotlight off the instructor. Rather than stressing the improvement of teaching, it looks to improve learning. It will frequently

1. For example, K. Patricia Cross, "On College Teaching," *Journal of Engineering Education* (Jan. 1983): 9–14. Kenneth A. Feldman, "The Superior College Teacher from the Students' View," *Research in Higher Education* 5 (1976): 43–88. Paul R. Pintrich, "A Process-Oriented View of Student Motivation and Cognition," in *Improving Teaching and Learning Through Research*, ed. J. S. Stark and L. A. Mets. New Directions for Institutional Research. No. 57. (San Francisco: Jossey-Bass, 1988), 65–79. K. Patricia Cross, "Classroom Research: Helping Professors Learn More About Teaching and Learning," in *How Administrators Can Improve Teaching*, ed. Peter Seldin and Associates. (San Francisco: Jossey-Bass, 1990), 122–42.

provide information that will enable us to help students change the way they try to learn. It also helps students to assess their own strengths and weaknesses and to become more involved in learning the course content. Also, students see that we are genuinely interested in helping them learn and not just in covering the material and in giving them a grade. Since classroom assessment is always within our control, we can use it to become more effective by helping to clarify our goals and priorities for the course and even for individual class sessions. It can also help us diagnose how well a particular lesson is working and invent different approaches. It is not surprising, then, that students tend to see classroom assessments as supportive and helpful teaching devices, not as threats or goads. Classroom assessment addresses the uniqueness of each class, since its sole purpose is to help this class do better. And we all know that what works for the 10:00 A.M., section may not work for the 2:00 P.M. section.

Classroom assessment is powerful because it gives the instructor an opportunity to give immediate feedback to students on how well they are doing so they do not have to wait until the midterm or final exam to get the bad news. And it gives the instructor instant feedback from the students that can lead to immediate changes in the course, so there is no need to wait until next year to introduce improvements. Best of all, effective classroom assessment techniques are available to every teacher. We don't need special training or a background in testing or statistics.

What It Takes

To get started using classroom assessment techniques, it helps if you build from success. It is best to experiment with classroom assessment for the first time in a course that is going well.

Second, it helps if you are willing to be flexible. Almost certainly, good classroom assessments will change the way a good teacher wants to teach the course. Old verities will suddenly not seem so certain, or at least not universally applicable. Lectures that you knew were the model of clarity and focus will oftentimes not seem so brilliant when it becomes evident how many students misunderstood their intent altogether.

Third, the whole process will be pointless if you are not willing to act on the basis of what you learn. A cardinal rule of classroom assessment is, "Don't ask the question if you don't want to know the answer." And that includes sharing what you learn with your students.

Assessment might reveal something that you can't or don't know how to deal with, and you are left frustrated knowing that there is a problem you cannot fix. In this case, it is important to share that frustration with your students and possibly your colleagues to see if together you can devise a solution.

Instructors in community colleges and research universities across the country are daily inventing and adapting classroom assessment techniques to meet the needs of their classes. Two of the national leaders who have done the most to propagate the benefits of classroom assessment and to bring together what we know about it are Thomas A. Angelo of American Association for Higher Education (AAHE) and K. Patricia Cross of the University of California, Berkeley. Their excellent annual summer institute at Berkeley has provided hundreds of teachers with a systematic introduction to assessment techniques and preparation to help their colleagues adopt classroom assessment. Their compendium, *Classroom Assessment Techniques: A Handbook for College Teachers* (1993),[2] provides a thorough and practical guide to anyone interested in taking up classroom assessment. Besides presenting very practical pedagogical advice, the book describes fifty assessment techniques and suggests how each could be adapted to fit the needs of different types of classes. A few examples from the Angelo and Cross handbook will suggest the ranges of these techniques.

One Minute Paper

An easy starter that is probably the most frequently used technique, and which is subject to countless variations, is the famous One Minute Paper (148–53). It provides quick and simple feedback to you and your students on what students have learned in a lecture or discussion. You simply finish the lesson three to five minutes before the end of the period, and in the time remaining ask the students to write on half-sheets of paper or on index cards the answer to two questions: "What was the most important thing you learned in this class?" and "What important question remains unanswered?" As students leave the room, they turn in these sheets anonymously. By

2. Much of the material of this article is drawn or adapted from this excellent handbook. Two videotapes demonstrate various assessment techniques and convey a feeling of how classroom assessment really works: *Classroom Research: Empowering Teachers*, Catalog No. 38022, University of California Extension Media Center; and *Teaching-Directed Classroom Research*, College of Marin.

looking quickly over the sheets after class, you can get a very quick picture of what students derived from the class and decide whether you want to spend any more time on that topic or to clarify points that students felt were still unclear. It is extremely important that you spend some time in the following class reporting back to the students what they had submitted and commenting on the responses in a general way to reinforce the main points and to correct commonly shared errors. Instructors often find that students raise better questions in the One Minute Paper than they do in class; so in responding to the most frequently asked questions, you have the opportunity to expand or clarify the most important points of the previous lecture. To prevent students from being disappointed that you did not respond to their particular question or comment on their response, it is useful for you to indicate in advance that you will have time to address only the most commonly asked questions.

For students, completing the One Minute Paper has a number of benefits. First, it requires students to review quickly the whole lecture and organize and evaluate what they have just heard; therefore, they need to become actively involved in using the material, even though they may be one of a few hundred students in the class. At the same time, if they know that at the end of the period they will be required to list a question that remains in their minds, they need to be thinking about what they understand and do not understand—again, a form of active involvement. Interestingly, teachers have found that if students anticipate having to complete a One Minute Paper, they begin to listen to the lectures in a more active manner and their responses tend to get better as the semester progresses. Even though the papers are not being graded and are turned in anonymously, students still tend to want to do a good job on them. By comparing their responses to those of other students in the class, they will quickly see that there were other points of view on the material. And, by hearing the feedback from you, the students will learn how an expert in the field assesses what was most important.

One of the beauties of the One Minute Paper is its flexibility. You can use it for lectures or discussions, as well as for laboratory sessions, films or videos, or field trips. One popular variation is the Muddiest Point (154–58) approach, in which you ask students to list what for them is still the muddiest point of the lecture they have just heard.[3]

3. See also F. Mosteller, "The 'Muddiest Point In The Lecture' As A Feedback Device," *On Teaching and Learning: The Journal of the Harvard-Danforth Center*, 3 (1989): 10–21.

Also, your questions can be tailored to fit the situation, to address a more specific question, or to challenge the students to integrate one lecture session with one that went before. When properly set up and administered, the One Minute Paper is welcomed by students because they realize that it helps them learn and, in a sense, have a voice in the class, even if they have not spoken.

Goal Ranking

A second very valuable classroom assessment technique is Goal Ranking and Matching (290–94). In the first week of class, you ask the students to list in priority order their three to five learning goals for the course. You should tell them that you will analyze the goals and report back and discuss the results. In this, as in all classroom assessments, you should have personally gone through the exercise previously. Also, should there be a wide discrepancy between what the students expect and what you intend to do, you must decide how much you are willing or able to adjust the course to meet student expectations. In many cases, you will want to use the occasion to clarify or articulate what the course is designed to accomplish and help students understand why it is that way. In other cases, you may be able to adapt the content or the teaching technique to approach more closely the student goals. It may be possible, for example, to enable some students to pursue their particular interests through a research project or term paper. If your course will not address the goals your students anticipated, they will appreciate knowing this early on, so they can drop your course and enroll in another.

Among the pedagogical advantages of the goal-ranking technique is the raising of awareness among students of the degree to which they have or do not have identifiable learning goals. It may provide an occasion for you to discuss how the course fits into the college's or the department's curriculum and how it relates to other courses. Also, if you discover that the students have a very high or very low personal investment in the course, that may suggest some special adaptations of the material or presentation. The student responses, unprompted or unprepared for, are likely to be very vague and thin—but even so, in the hands of a skilled instructor they can provide a learning moment for the students, if they can be led to take a more active and involved approach to their own education.

Memory Matrix

A third very flexible technique can be thoroughly integrated into the teaching process, especially in introductory courses. The Memory Matrix (142–47) is a very simple procedure that enables you to see how well your students recall some basic information and are able to analyze and organize or categorize the material.[4] You develop a grid, with vertical columns headed by major concepts or areas that define the material and horizontal rows of different concepts or categories. You ask students to write in the appropriate cells the items that fit under the major concepts: you can furnish the list of items to be categorized, or you can ask your students to supply them themselves.

Cross and Angelo (1993) present an example of the Memory Matrix which could be used in an art history class. The students fill in the appropriate cells with the names of the major artists the class has studied.

	France	United States	Great Britain
Neoclassicism			
Impressionism			
Postimpressionism			
Expressionism			

Source: Thomas Angelo and Patricia K. Cross, "Memory Matrix," in *Classroom Assessment Technique: A Handbook for College Teachers,* 2d ed. (San Francisco: Jossey-Bass, 1993), 143. Courtesy Jossey-Bass, Inc.

Having asked the class to complete the matrix themselves, the instructor could then divide the class into small groups to try to pool their memory. She would be able to discover, for example, whether or not the students could easily identify the country of the artists and distinguish Impressionists from Postimpressionists and so on. As part

4. See also "Categorizing Grid," 160–63, and "Defining Features Matrix," 164–67.

of her feedback the instructor could explain why art historians categorize artists in this fashion and why it is not always clear where an
individual belongs. On a practical level she can help students prepare
for their final exam. As an alternative approach, she could use the
matrix as an in-class teaching exercise using an overhead projector
and filling in the missing information provided by the class.

Clearly, the Memory Matrix can be an effective teaching tool as
well as an assessment technique, especially in courses introducing
large amounts of material that students are seeing for the first time.
Also, it is a device that students can adapt to use on their own to help
organize other material in their minds.

Everyday Ethical Dilemma

A variety of assessment tools focus on students' attitudes and values, which for some fields can be extremely important but problematic
to handle in the classroom. It is sometimes difficult or misleading to
try to read students' personal attitudes from their class discussions.
The force of a strongly articulated view can skew discussion among
students groping to clarify their own value systems. Some students
are silent or extremely circumspect; others say what they believe to
be socially or politically acceptable. One technique that provides an
excellent teaching device as well as a useful assessment of student
values is the presentation of an Everyday Ethical Dilemma (271–74).

In an Everyday Ethical Dilemma, you have students write briefly
and anonymously their response to an ethical dilemma relevant to the
course. The challenge to the students is that they must clarify their
own values by thinking through a brief hypothetical situation you
present. You analyze the responses and report back to the class the
various views they have presented. You are able to identify the patterns that appear, in order to help students see the differences among
themselves and the implications of each position. Discussion or argument may follow, ideally leading to students' increased recognition of
the various value systems found in the class as well as various perceptions of the facts presented in the case. From the written responses to
this hypothetical case, you get honest statements from all the students
(not just the dominant personalities) and are therefore better able to
address the whole class in responding and in teaching subsequent
material.

Ethical dilemmas are more frequently useful in professional fields
such as social work, nursing, or education or in liberal disciplines such
as philosophy. But they also can prove useful in first-year seminars

orienting students to college life. One instructor, for example, presented her first year students with a hypothetical case of Anne, whose roommate, Barbara, confided to her that she was planning to help her boyfriend cheat on an exam. The assessment asked students to respond to the question "What would you do if you were Anne?" and to explain their reasons. When the instructor analyzed the responses (the majority of which were that they would do nothing about the cheating), it provided the occasion for vigorous discussion of academic integrity.

Applications Cards

A fifth example of possible assessment techniques is Applications Cards (236–39), in which, very simply, students write on an index card at least one realistic application of the general principle or theory they have just learned. This technique forces students to think actively about the material and to connect it with what they already know. The pedagogical value of focusing on the practical value of the lesson is clear.

Here are some examples of ways in which instructors have used this device. In an economics class studying Gresham's law, "good money drives out bad," students were asked to give at least one example besides money of a situation in which Gresham's law applies. In physics, students were introduced to Newton's Third Law, "to every action there is always an equal and opposite reaction," and then were asked to list three applications of the law to everyday life. In political science, one of the standard maxims of American political history is that "all politics is local"; students were challenged to imagine that they were giving advice to a presidential candidate and to apply this principle.

In sorting out the responses and commenting on them in the next class you will be able to distinguish for the class those responses that were excellent from those that were just acceptable and from those that were not acceptable. One of the pedagogical advantages of this technique is that students can learn from hearing the best examples pointed out to them. Tom Angelo suggests, in this and other instances, that you disguise somewhat those responses you intend to criticize or reject.

Helpful Lessons

From instructors' experiments with assessment techniques, a number of lessons have emerged that help assure success. First, identify a question you would like to know the answer to; that is, the answer to the question will assist you in conducting the class and improving student learning. A very common question is "How well do my students understand _____?" Second, at the start, be as sure as you can be in advance that your assessment technique will be seen as a positive experience by the students while providing you the information you are seeking. Not all techniques are appropriate for your class. Use only those that are. Third, jump into classroom assessment slowly. Start with small, manageable techniques, such as the One Minute Paper, and develop the style that works for you. Fourth, set limits on how much out-of-class and in-class time you are willing to invest. Fifth, always close the communication circle by giving feedback to the students—not just what they wrote but your reaction to it or analysis of it. In some instances, you may want to let the class know that you will be departing from the original class schedule or syllabus in response to what you learned from the assessment (25–32, 58–59).[5]

Costs and Benefits

As with every change in the way we do our business, there are costs and presumably there are benefits. Users of classroom assessments report that there are three major costs incurred in introducing the technique:[6] (1) It takes time in and out of class; that can mean more work for you and less time in class to cover the material. (2) Taking time to do assessments and assuring that the class understands the material can force you to cover fewer things; hence, the coverage of the course content is reduced and some items, presumably less important, must be curtailed or dropped. (3) You may become frustrated after you learn something from assessments that you can do nothing about—whether that is students' prior academic deficiencies, their life styles, or the department's curricular shortcomings.

5. See also AAHE Assessment Forum, "Principles of Good Practice for Assessing Learning" (Washington, D.C.: American Association for Higher Education, 1992).

6. Diana K. Kelly, "Classroom Assessment for Adult Learners," paper presented at Classroom Research Institute, Univ. of California, Berkeley, Aug. 11–14, 1993. Diana K. Kelly, Michelle Miller, and Michelle Wilder, "Increasing Involvement in Learning with Classroom Assessment," in *Knowing: The Power of Stories*, ed. Philip H. Dreyer. Fifty-fifth Yearbook of the Claremont Reading Conference, 1991. Thomas A. Angelo, "Ten Easy Pieces: Assessing Higher Learning in Four Dimensions," *Classroom Research: Early Lessons From Success*, New Directions for Teaching and Learning No. 46 (San Francisco: Jossey-Bass, 1991) 17–31.

On the other hand, users tend to find three very powerful benefits that follow the systematic use of assessment techniques. (1) Students tend to respond very positively to the constructive use of these techniques, when they see the techniques benefit them and they experience the excitement and interest the techniques can generate in a class. They see these techniques as evidence of your genuine concern and a type of cooperation between you and the class. In some instances, having experienced assessments in one class, students have asked other instructors who did not use classroom assessment why they did not. (2) For many instructors, assessment has pumped fresh excitement into a course that had grown tired and stale. When students become more actively involved in the course and begin to feel a sense of ownership, which assessment invites, the course does begin to change in the eyes of instructor and students alike. Assessment can make the classroom a more engaging place to be on either side of the desk. (3) When several colleagues take the plunge at one time, collegial interaction can become enriched. Swapping notes and suggestions can open new fields of conversation among you and your fellow instructors. Brown-bag lunches, for example, for instructors interested in classroom assessment can be extremely enjoyable since the techniques open up new styles of teaching that are interesting to discuss.

Conclusion

One of the most attractive aspects of using classroom assessment techniques is that they can be used in large and small classes, on an occasional basis or in a manner that integrates them into the course structure. Ultimately, however, they all lead in the same direction: toward a redefinition of the student-instructor relationship and the role of the instructor in the classroom. Using classroom assessments can contribute to an atmosphere supporting active and collaborative learning, and a more open and responsive teaching style. Ultimately, it helps answer the most important question that every instructor must ask. Not "How well am I teaching?" but "How well are my students learning?" and "How can we together improve their performance?"

8

Using Writing as an Active Learning Tool

DUANE H. ROEN AND KENNETH J. LINDBLOM

A first-year college or university writing course is not an inoculation against illiteracy; a second course is not a booster shot. Learning to write is a life-long journey that begins even before the child can hold a pencil.[1]

Students entering a college or university should have had considerable guided writing experience in high school, middle school, elementary school, and even preschool. Students should view a first-semester course as a site where they acquire additional tools and strategies for becoming more effective writers. In the course, they gain practice at invention, drafting, revising (which focuses on content), and editing (which focuses on surface features of their texts). Students learn that feedback on their writing should come throughout the process of composing, and they should understand that feedback early in the process is generally more effective than feedback coming later. In a first-semester course, they also should have considerable practice using writing as a tool for learning, for becoming engaged with course content. This informal writing practice includes numerous course journals and learning logs, written dialogues, annotations in margins of books, double-entry notebooks, and flow charts. Further, students should share this informal writing so that they can challenge one another's thinking. The goal should be to encourage students to use language more consciously and more strategically as

1. This chapter grows out of a series of active-learning workshops that we conducted for teaching assistants at Syracuse University during Fall 1993.

they write and speak in their academic, professional, and personal lives.

Most of you reading this chapter are not writing teachers. Most of you teach in the content areas of science, mathematics, social science, business, engineering, humanities, and fine arts. The courses that you teach offer students opportunities to enter the discourse communities of your various disciplines—something their writing instructors cannot do for them as easily. Long-standing members of discourse communities are best equipped to lead students into those communities, and these long-standing members are, of course, professors, part-time instructors, and teaching assistants in the disciplines. Work in the most effective courses includes the kinds of writing that encourage students to think in disciplinary ways as physicists, mathematicians, historians, and artists think as they do their work. Some of that writing should be formal, some informal. Some should be used to present information; some should help learners engage discipline-specific material. In these courses, as in others, writing promotes learning the content, without taking time away from it. Any college or university community should understand that students need to write progressively more as they move further into their majors. When they graduate, students should feel confident maneuvering both as readers and as writers through the discourse of various disciplines, especially their own. Such confidence results from much guided practice. And the students' writing can act as a guide for instructors.

Consider student writing a window into the thought processes of your students; these windows allow you to gauge your teaching according to the students' actual needs. If a math instructor asks her students to explain a calculus problem in words on paper, she can see the students' thought in action and can indicate the places where their thinking may be going awry. Rather than reteach an entire process, this instructor can simply point out the one spot (or several spots, as the case may be) where the student needs to concentrate, and help the student take a major leap in his or her math skills. This is only one instance where using informal writing can actually cut down on time taken away from learning new content.

For several reasons this chapter focuses on informal kinds of writing, rather than formal ones such as essays. First, it is virtually impossible to do much with formal writing in one chapter. For those of you interested in more formal kinds of writing in the disciplines, you might peruse the list of suggested reading provided. Second, the kinds of informal writing described in this chapter can do much to actively engage students in their course material in any discipline.

Some instructors mistakenly think that enriching their curriculum with informal writing will add tremendous amounts of time to their already overwhelming workload. This need not be the case. In fact, as the calculus example above illustrates, using informal writing in class can actually make teaching more efficient by keeping instructors and their students better informed about what the students have learned and how they have grown as thinkers. Concerns about an increased workload usually stem from the myth that an instructor must grade or respond to every word that students write for the written work to be useful to them. After all, that myth suggests, why make students write if they're not going to get credit for it? And why assign writing if you don't plan to grade it or in some cases even read it? Actually there are compelling reasons for both.

By now, you may already be clear about how writing that has never been handed in can be useful to students; they can read the writing aloud in class, or use the writing to spark small-group discussion. Beyond those practical in-class uses of writing there is an even more compelling reason for asking your students to write regularly. Often we think of using writing only as a way of allowing students to express what they already know. This kind of writing, what the British writing theorist James Britton calls "transactional" writing, may seem to end logically with a grade and feedback from the instructor, telling the students where they went right and where they went wrong. There are other kinds of writing, though, that do not have as their purpose to show what the writer already knows. This kind of writing, what many writing teachers call "writing to learn," gives students experience as thinkers in the disciplines in which the writing is assigned. An instructor who assigns writing to learn asks students to try to think like a physicist or sociologist or composer of music. Such writing assignments provide students with real, practical experience in a discipline and can actually be thought of as mini-internships. Consider the instructor who says to her students, "For the next fifteen minutes of class, I would like you to be chemists. We have just completed this experiment, which you have never seen or heard of before, though we have used chemicals and techniques with which you have become somewhat familiar. Write about what you think may have happened to give us the results we just got." The students in that chemistry instructor's class spend fifteen minutes thinking about and trying to understand chemistry, acting as chemists. They use writing not as a means to show others what they already know, but rather as a means to incorporate their previous knowledge with their developing skills of analysis and the specifics of the experiment they just completed. This instructor isn't asking her students to *pretend* to be chemists, but rather she is providing them the opportunity to *be* chemists, allowing them to figure out for themselves, using their own skills as analyzers and logical thinkers, what just happened in the experiment they observed. Those who are able to figure out the results of the experiment will exercise and hone their skills as chemists, while those who don't discover the results will enjoy the benefit of learning from their experience of making mistakes as chemists. And another benefit when chemists experiment in writing there's little danger of blowing up a lab!

When instructors choose to read and respond to student writing, there are again two models they can follow: they may evaluate or grade the writing, or they may simply respond to the writing. While transactional writing may seem to require a grade and instructor commentary on its quality, there are more beneficial modes of response that can be used for transactional writing and writing to learn. Two writing teachers at the State University of New York at Albany, Cy Knoblauch and Lil Brannon (1982), split commentary into two modes: "directive" and "facilitative." Directive commentary is feedback from an instructor that checks off for students what they have done right and what they have done wrong and explains how they should proceed. Such directive or prescriptive response is less useful, say Knoblauch and Brannon, than facilitative commentary, which treats the student writing as legitimate inquiry. Consider again our chemistry teacher who asked her students to spend fifteen minutes trying to discover in writing how the result of the experiment came about. It would not be very useful to the student who actually thought on paper to be graded on how well he thought. Rather, facilitative feedback from the instructor would ask questions in the margins of the student's writing that would lead him or her to inquire further. In giving feedback on writing to learn, the instructor's goal should not be to end the exercise but be to continue the students' inquiry into the discipline. This chemistry teacher's commentary might be marked by such questions, as "Have you considered the role of the catalyst in this phase of the experiment?" or "What other ways might this element of the experiment that you've pointed out function in the experiment?" or "What steps might you have left out at this stage in the experiment?" Treating the student as a coinquirer through the use of facilitative commentary has benefits even beyond teaching students course content. When students think of themselves as members of the discipline, their work often rises to that level. Conversely, constant overly directive commentary places the student in a "subordinate thinker" role and can actually shut down student thought processes and end real growth.

The rest of this chapter offers some well-traveled informal writing tasks. The list is representative but by no means exhaustive of the kinds of informal writing that can actively engage students in course content. Where an activity is described without an example that a student has written, consider developing examples in your own disciplines—examples that you can share with your students as you help them use writing to become more active learners in your classes.

Admit Slip

Admit slips are very short pieces of writing that you collect at the door at the beginning of class. You could have your students write on admit slips any of the following: questions that students have about the assigned reading for the day, questions about the material covered in the previous class session, or a one-sentence summary of an important point from the reading or the previous class session. After collecting these, you could read some of them aloud to initiate a class discussion, or you might want to speak to each question or summary. Admit slips encourage active learning because they give voice to many more students than is typically the case in classrooms where all instructor-student and student-student interactions are oral, rather than a combination of written and oral.

In a physics class for nonmajors, one instructor asked students to turn in an admit slip with a response to the following prompt: "Explain the law of conservation of matter and energy in your own words and provide a practical example of how the law functions." One student wrote the following:

> The law of conservation of matter and energy means that we can't produce anything that wasn't already there, nor can we get rid of anything that is already there. All we can do is change how matter and energy looks or behaves.
>
> One practical example of how the law can be important is in the winter. When snow piles up on a roof, some people worry that when the snow begins to melt, it will get heavier and collapse the roof. Actually, as the law states, the same amount of matter (and weight) is on the roof when the snow melts as when the snow is not melting.

So if the weight of the snow didn't collapse the roof, neither will the weight of the melting snow.

Exit Slip

Exit slips differ from admit slips only in that you collect them at the end of a class session rather than the beginning, and they require some time in class. It is important that you provide time for in-class writing, as it demonstrates to students your commitment to using writing as a tool for active learning. For an exit slip, you might give students the last five minutes of class to answer a specific question, summarize the lesson, indicate points of confusion, or solve a problem by applying the day's major concept. By collecting the slips at the end of a class period, you have more time to analyze, synthesize, or evaluate what students have written. In turn, you can use the information gleaned from the slips to plan or modify the subsequent lesson, especially if the slips indicate a consistent pattern of misunderstanding.

Dialectical Learning Log Entries

The word *dialectical* is related to the word *dialectic*, which is a method for getting at the truth by comparing/contrasting two sides of an issue. The philosopher Hegel (1967) treated dialectic as the examination of a thesis, an antithesis, and a resulting synthesis to solve a problem or to analyze an idea.

Many people have found dialectical learning log entries among the most effective strategies for reflecting on ideas—especially ideas found in reading materials. To do a dialectical learning log entry as Berthoff (1982) suggests, describe the instructions to your students as follows: "You first need to draw a vertical line down the middle of a page or a screen. At the top of the left half of the page, write the heading Reading Notes. At the top on the right side, write the heading Comments and Questions. Above these two headings you may wish to note the date of the entry so you can keep track of the history of your thinking. You also should make some bibliographic notes, so you don't forget which piece of reading is the subject of your entry. This is a good way to practice following a style sheet. Researchers use these notes to build their works cited/reference lists to avoid backtracking later.

You may wish to record reading notes on the left side of the page while you read or after you have read the piece once. Or you may wish to do both. The advantage of recording notes while you're reading is that you are able to record ideas while they are fresh in your mind.

Dialectical Log Entry

Reading   ——————————————————— Date   ————

       Reading Notes   Comments/Questions

The guiding principle for writing comments and questions on the right side of the page is to jot them down as they occur to you. You will find that your comments and questions will appear at all sorts of times. Some of them, of course, will occur as you read, before you even record a reading note on the left side of the page. Some of them will occur as you are writing a note. Others may occur to you as you are listening to a class lecture or participating in a discussion. And still others may occur at odd moments: while walking to school, while eating dinner, while lying in bed. Whenever they occur, though, you need to catch them before they slip away, perhaps forever. Above you will find a blank dialectical log entry. It will give you a visual image to guide you as you create your own entries.

Dialectical log entries demonstrate that readers are actually in dialogue with the texts they read. The entries indicate the places where the texts coincide or resonate with a reader's previous experience, and those are the "places" where learning from text begins to be most effective. If you read your students' dialectical log entries, although it is not necessary, you can learn quite a bit about how they engage with the texts you assign to them.

Here is an entry that a student did as he or she was beginning to read Thomas Kuhn's *The Structure of Scientific Revolutions* (1970).

Dialectical Log Entry

Reading ___Structure of Scientific Revolutions___ Date ___02/19/94___

Reading Notes	Comments/Questions
"Attempting to discover the source of that difference led me to recognize scientific achievements that for a time provide model problems and solutions to a community of practitioners" (p. viii).	Here Kuhn says that paradigms are used by their respective communities (fields, I suppose). I think it is important to note that Kuhn, when studying with behavioral scientists (social scientists) was struck by many disagreements betw. the social scientists that concerned the nature of legit. scientific problems. Kuhn admits that natural scientists probably do not have a better hold on the answers than do the social scientists. Because of this, Kuhn has delved into the paradigm, in an attempt to discover why there existed such a great difference between the social scientists and natural scientists.
". . . there are circumstances though I think them rare, under which two paradigms can coexist peacefully in the later period" (p. ix).	This might be important later.

The student's reactions to Kuhn's opening remarks may not accurately reflect Kuhn's thinking; indeed, Kuhn says so little about the social sciences in his book that we must conclude that the student is guessing at what must have gone through Kuhn's mind. What is important here, though, is that the student is using the entry to explore his own "reading" of Kuhn's ideas.

Biopoem

For at least the last decade or so writing teachers have known about the power of the biopoem (biographical poem) to help students understand certain types of course material. Recently, Ann Ruggles

Gere (1985), a writing scholar at the University of Michigan, published accounts of how students in history, English, and science have used biopoems to learn those subjects more thoroughly. The biopoem looks like this:

Line 1: First name
Line 2: Four traits that describe the character
Line 3: Relative of _____
Line 4: Lover of _____ (list several people or things)
Line 5: Who feels _____ (several things)
Line 6: Who needs _____ (several things)
Line 7: Who fears _____ (several things)
Line 8: Who gives _____ (several things)
Line 9: Who would like to see _____ (several things)
Line 10: Resident of _____
Line 11: Last name

The assigned form makes it easier to write a biopoem because then students can think more about content and less about how to shape that content. The first time you and your students use the biopoem in class, you might make it autobiographical. Doing so lets everyone think and write about a topic they know very well. Here's an example written by one of the authors of this chapter:

Duane,
middle-aged, Norwegian, "stinky-winky";
Father of Nicholas James and Hanna Elizabeth;
Who loves family history, softball, furniture restoration, carpentry, and woodworking;
Who feels fortunate to be healthy and proud to be a teacher;
Who needs more time for his children, more energy for his work, and more opportunities to see his Grandma Bennett;
Who fears that life will pass him by, that Garrison Keillor's show will never again be broadcast in Syracuse, and that his scholarship will decline;
Who gives time to his colleagues and students, much thought to his decisions, and a full commitment to his job;
Who would like to see all of his ancestors, peace in the world, and an end to all pain and suffering;
Resident of cloudy and wet Syracuse;
Roen.

This sample biopoem is personal; Duane sometimes writes biopoems with students on the first day of class to get to know them better and to let them get to know him better. But the biopoem has many applications that promote learning course content. Students can write biopoems about literary characters, historical figures, and people in the news. But students also can use the biopoem to breathe some life into an idea, theory, event, place, object, and the like. To give the form a try, you might use it to write about some well-known person, event, and concept in your own field. The form encourages students to think in ways that they have never thought before.

Dialogue

A dialogue, in the simplest terms possible, is a dialogic transaction between/among people, ideas, or concepts. In most classrooms, there are many dialogues among students and between students and instructor. Intellectual dialogues can, as Plato's Socratic dialogues exemplify, do much to enhance understanding. Perhaps the easiest kind of course-content dialogue to write is one between two persons, ideas, or concepts that seem to be at nearly complete odds, for example, Ptolemy and Johannes Kepler on the nature of the universe, President Lincoln and General McClellan on military strategy, Socrates (Plato) and Gorgias on the nature of knowledge and truth, Mozart and Beethoven on their processes of composing, Marxism and capitalism, romanticists and postmodernists. By asking students to create imaginary dialogues between such entities, you encourage them to examine those entities. As a result, they often tease out subtleties that they might otherwise ignore. In the late 1970s, Steve Allen created and hosted the television series *Meeting of Minds,* which had episodes that collected in dialogue such diverse notables as Martin Luther, Voltaire, Plato, and Florence Nightingale (episode 9).

Students in an introductory music course might be asked to write a dialogue between Mozart and Beethoven, comparing their composing processes. What writing the dialogue does for the students is encourage them to put contrasting ideas in direct contact and engage with those ideas in their own language. The instructor might ask several students to read their imaginary dialogues to the whole class. Then the instructor might ask everyone to discuss features of each dialogue that best capture the nature of Mozart's and Beethoven's composing. As a group, the class might even synthesize all of the dialogues into one that they agree best represents the two legends' composing.

Unsent Letter

An unsent letter is, as the name suggests, a letter that is unsent. The possibilities for its use are almost limitless. Students might, for example, write, as themselves, to the literary characters or the historical figures that they are studying. Alternatively, they might adopt the personae of these characters and figures to write letters: e.g., Antigone writing to her father, Oedipus, to express her feelings about the curse that he brought upon the family; Grant writing to Lee the day before the surrender at Appomatox; Einstein writing to Newton to explain how their theories of motion differ; Sitting Bull writing to George Custer *after* the Battle of the Little Bighorn; a Vietnam M.I.A. writing to a conscientious objector; Leonardo da Vinci writing to his painting *Mona Lisa* to express his feelings for the work; Salvador Dali writing to a realist painter to explain his views of art; Galileo writing to Copernicus to explain why he denounced the latter's model of the solar system—you get the idea.

Time Line/Chronology

A time line is nothing more than a chronological list of ideas, events, people. For example, a student in an introductory art history course might make a chronological list of Van Gogh's paintings in an effort to determine for himself what patterns of development might exist there. To complicate the process, he might construct two parallel time lines one listing Van Gogh's paintings, the other listing major events in the artist's emotional life. By comparing the two lists, he can begin to see literally relationships between Van Gogh's work and his emotions. This kind of activity would certainly encourage the student to study the paintings and writings of Van Gogh in more detail which is exactly what the art history instructor hoped would happen.

Flowchart

A flowchart is a visual representation of the relationships among ideas, or events. Here, for example, is a flowchart that a student in an introductory course in the history of science constructed to help her make sense of Thomas Kuhn's explanation of paradigmatic change in science.

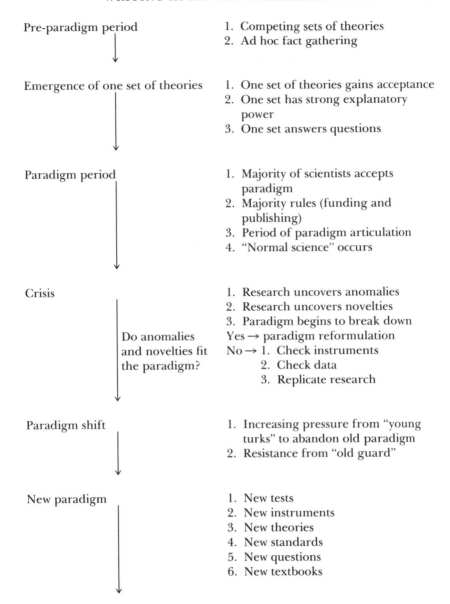

Pre-paradigm period

1. Competing sets of theories
2. Ad hoc fact gathering

Emergence of one set of theories

1. One set of theories gains acceptance
2. One set has strong explanatory power
3. One set answers questions

Paradigm period

1. Majority of scientists accepts paradigm
2. Majority rules (funding and publishing)
3. Period of paradigm articulation
4. "Normal science" occurs

Crisis

1. Research uncovers anomalies
2. Research uncovers novelties
3. Paradigm begins to break down

Do anomalies and novelties fit the paradigm?

Yes → paradigm reformulation
No → 1. Check instruments
2. Check data
3. Replicate research

Paradigm shift

1. Increasing pressure from "young turks" to abandon old paradigm
2. Resistance from "old guard"

New paradigm

1. New tests
2. New instruments
3. New theories
4. New standards
5. New questions
6. New textbooks

On the left side, the students simply lists the stages of paradigm shifts that Kuhn discusses in a book-length essay. On the right side, he or she numbers some defining features for each stage. The flowchart may oversimplify Kuhn's theory of change, but it is useful because it helps the student understand some complex thinking.

Genealogy

A genealogy is, literally, a pedigree chart tracing the ancestry of a concept, idea, paradigm, or, of course, a person. There are some obvious uses of genealogies in history courses, but the technique is useful in other contexts, as well. A student in a literature course for example, constructed a genealogy of the characters in the Oedipus cycle, beginning by piecing together details from the plays themselves. To augment that information, the student consulted *Lempriere's Classical Dictionary*. The activity helped the student to understand familial relationships among Sophocles's characters and some figures not mentioned in the plays.

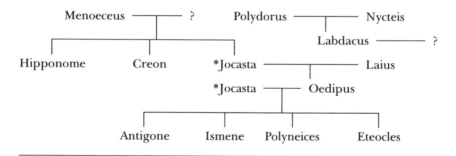

*Jocasta is both the mother and wife of Oedipus. She is, therefore, both the grandmother and mother of Antigone, Ismene, Polyneices, and Eteocles.

Resume/Curriculum Vitae

The term curriculum vitae is Latin for "the course of one's life." It is often abbreviated as CV. Most likely you will have already constructed your own CV. Writing a resume or CV for an historical figure can help put that person's life and work into perspective. It works even more effectively if the writer can imagine himself or herself to be the historical figure. A student reading a book such as Banesh Hoffman's *Albert Einstein: Creator and Rebel* (1972), for example, might develop the following CV for Einstein:

CURRICULUM VITAE
Albert Einstein

Personal Information

Born: March 14, 1879; Ulm, Germany	(p. 11)
Sister: Maja (1881–1951)	(p. 242)
Married to Mileva Maric in 1903	(p. 39)
Divorced in 1919	(p. 134)
Mileva died in 1948 in Zurich	(p. 240)
Children:	
Hans Albert, born 1904	(p. 39)
Eduard, born 1910	(p. 39)
Married to Elsa Einstein (distant cousin) in 1919	(p. 134)
(Elsa died in 1936)	(p. 230)
Children:	
Ilse	(p. 250)
Margot	(p. 250)
U.S. Citizenship: Oct. 1, 1935	(p. 234)
Death: April 18, 1955; Princeton	(p. 261)

Awards, Honors

1913: Elected to Royal Prussian Academy of Science	(p. 100)
1921: Nobel Prize for Physics (photoelectric effect)	(p. 54)
1921: Honorary Degree Princeton University	(p. 145)
1925: Gold Medal Royal Astronomical Society of London	(pp. 135, 253)
1929: Planck Medal	(p. 157)

Education

1885–1889: Catholic Elementary School Munich	(p. 16)
1885–1893: Violin Lessons	(p. 20)
1889–1894: Luitpold Gymnasium (high school), Munich	(p. 19)
1896–1900: Federal Institute of Technology, Zurich	(p. 27)
1905: Ph.D., University of Zurich	(p. 55)

Positions

1902–1909: Swiss Patent Office	(p. 35)
1902–1906: Technical Expert Third Class	(pp. 35, 82)
1906–1909: Technical Expert Second Class	(pp. 82, 87)
1908: Bern University	(p. 87)
Privatdozent	(p. 87)
1909–1911: Zurich University	(p. 88)
Associate Professor of Theoretical Physics	(p. 88)
1911–1912: German University, Prague Full	
Professor	(p. 94)
1912–1914: Federal Institute of Technology,	
Zurich Professor	(p. 100)
1914–1933: Kaiser Wilhelm Institute Berlin	(pp. 100, 167)
Director	
1930–1931: California Institute of Technology	(p. 159)
Visiting Professor	
1933: Institute for Advanced Study Princeton	(p. 170)

Selected Publications

1906: "A New Determination of the Sizes of	
Molecules", *Annalen der Physik*	(pp. 55, 56)
1907: $E = mc^2$: paper,	
Jahrbuch der Radioaktivitat	(p. 81)
1915: *The Foundations of the General Theory of*	
Relativity	(p. 130)
1921: *The Meaning of Relativity*, Princeton	
University Press.	(p. 146)

Selected Addresses

1909: "The Development of Our View of the	
Nature and Constitution of Radiation,"	
Eighty-First Congress of German Scientists	
and Physicians, Salzburg.	(p. 93)
1930: Paper offering proposal for	
circumventing Heisenberg's indeterminacy	
principle, Sixth Solvay Congress, Brussels	(p. 190)
1933, "On the Method of Theoretical Physics,"	
Oxford	(p. 170)

Personal Index

A personal index is an individual reader's index to a book. It is a guide to what information the reader found useful and/or important. A great place to keep such an index is inside the front and/or back cover. It helps the reader later find material in a book; when writing a course paper or preparing for exams.

One student read anthropologist Clifford Geertz's book *Local Knowledge* (1983) and generated the personal index excerpted below:

intellectual poaching license (p. 21)
society as game, drama, or text (p. 23)
"life is just a bowl of strategies." (p. 25)
social life as drama (pp. 26-)
social life as text (pp. 30-)
thought as product and process (p. 151).

Looking at your students' personal indexes will further acquaint you with their thought processes, especially by noting what students understand to be important in a reading of a text.

Marginal Annotations

Marginal annotations are questions or comments written in the margins of a book. Like a personal index, these help readers highlight and personalize information. You might suggest to your students that each page of a book have at least one note, but preferably more. In fact, one of the authors of this chapter likes to say that he is so used to writing marginal notes on books that he cannot read without a pen in his hand. Don't hesitate to assign the writing of marginal comments whenever you assign reading to your students.

We all know that some students sell some of their books back to the campus bookstore at the end of the semester, and so are sometimes reluctant to write in their books. If that is the case, you could have students construct a personal index and make their marginal annotations on separate sheets of paper, in a notebook, or on computer disk.

Mnemonic Play

Mnemonic play involves creating mnemonic devices to help organize or remember information. For example, elementary school children sometimes remember the order of the planets in our solar system by using a sentence in which the first letter of each word corresponds to the first letter of each of the planets: "My very educated mother just served us nine pizzas." The sentence works so well because it exploits the psychological principle of chunking. That is, information is easier to hold in memory if it can be grouped. In this case the nine chunks of information—Mercury, Venus, Earth, Mars, Jupiter, Saturn, Uranus, Neptune, Pluto—get combined into one chunk, a single sentence. Remember the sentence, and you remember the names of the nine planets in order of their distance from the sun.

When you talk with students about mnemonic play, the best advice may be to make certain that it is a form of play. Encourage them to find clever and fun ways of chunking information so that it's more memorable to them, and spend some time in class designing mnemonics with students to help them learn that skill. It will serve them well.

Summary

The important thing to understand is that students learn and understand in many different ways. Informal writing can help them learn more quickly and more efficiently, so in the hands of a creative instructor it is a method that is rich with possibility. Use writing often in and out of class, and you will engage students more intensely in the course content.

To end this chapter, here's an example of the kind of handout that you might give to students on the first day of class so that they will have a sense of how to use informal writing to enhance their learning of course content.

Ideas for a Course Journal or Learning Log

1. If a passage strikes some chord in you, stop to free write about it. You might start with the emotional response that the passage evokes.

2. Write a letter to an historical figure. In that letter, you might tell him or her about another figure's actions or thoughts.

3. Write a hypothetical conversation that you might have with a contemporary or historical figure. (See #2 for possible topics.)

4. Write a biographical poem about a contemporary or historical figure. See page 76 for an example of a biopoem.

5. Write a hypothetical conversation between two historical figures.

6. List the personality traits of each figure.

7. Write a letter to the author to tell him or her what you like and dislike about the textbook.

8. Place an historical or contemporary figure in another setting or situation. For example, place General McClellan (Mr. Indecision) at the Battle of Agincourt in 1415. Describe how the figure would act in that new setting. Explain why he or she would act that way.

9. Pretend that you will make a film about a particular historical event. How would you cast the film? Where would you film it? What sorts of shots (camera angle, distance, lens) would you use for some particular scene(s)?

10. Free write about specific events or figures described in your textbook.

11. List questions that occur to you as you read or after you have read. Bring those questions to class for discussion.

12. Does the figure or event remind you of other figures or events? If so, describe the similarities.

13. Adopt the persona of an historical figure; write a letter to another figure. Two classmates might do this together, each writing to the other.

14. Write a dialogue in which you introduce an historical figure to a friend of yours.

15. Take some special interest that you have—your major hobby, for example—and use some system of analysis from that special interest to analyze some feature of a figure or event.

16. Take on the persona of a figure; write a diary entry.

17. Use metaphors to describe a figure or event.

18. Retell an event or describe a figure to a child and/or an adult who knows little about the event or figure.

19. Make a timeline for a series of events.

20. Rewrite the event into an episode for a soap opera.

Ways to Use Log/Journal Entries Once Students Have Generated Them

1. Ask several students to read entries at the beginning of class. Those entries might serve as the basis for that day's discussion. Of course, you will need to plan to use specific kinds of entries to generate specific kinds of discussions.

2. Ask students to do a specific kind of entry before they come to class. At the beginning of class, in a large group, give students very specific instructions for using the entries in small groups.

3. Respond in writing to certain entries to help students see how the entries can lead to their critical essays. Here, of course, you may use both comments and questions.

4. Ask questions in each student's log to encourage him or her to do certain kinds of additional entries.

5. Use the last five minutes of class to have students synthesize the day's discussion.

6. Ask students to write log entries to summarize or synthesize the work they did in small groups on a particular day.

7. Ask two students to exchange logs to respond to each other's entries.

Suggested Readings

This short bibliography should help you find other ways to encourage your students to use writing to make learning more meaningful. Note that the list includes books for instructors who work with high school and even elementary school students. Ideas usually translate easily from one level to another. Doing the work of such translation is a great way to reflect on your own teaching practices.

Biddle, Arthur, and Daniel Bean. 1987. *Writer's Guide: Life Sciences.* Lexington, Mass.: D. C. Heath.

Biddle, Arthur, and Kenneth Holland. 1987. *Writer's Guide: Political Science.* Lexington, Mass.: D. C. Heath.

Bizzell, Patricia, and Bruce Herzberg. 1986. "Writing Across the Curriculum: A Bibliographic Essay," 340–84. In *The Territory of Language: Linguistics, Stylistics, and the Teaching of Composition,* 2d ed, edited by Donald McQuade. Carbondale: Southern Illinois Univ. Press.

Bond, Lynne, and Anthony Magistrale. 1987. *Writer's Guide: Psychology.* Lexington, Mass.: D. C. Heath.

Brown, Stuart C., Robert K. Mittan, and Duane H. Roen. 1990. *Becoming Expert: Writing and Learning in the Disciplines.* Dubuque, Iowa: Kendall/Hunt.

Clegg, Cyndia Susan. 1988. *Critical Reading and Writing Across the Disciplines.* New York: Holt, Rinehart and Winston.

Connolly, Paul, and Teresa Vilardi, eds. 1989. *Writing to Learn Mathematics and Science.* New York: Teachers College Press.

Fulwiler, Toby, and Art Young, eds. 1982. *Language Connections: Writing and*

Reading Across the Curriculum. Urbana, Ill.: National Council of Teachers of English.

Fulwiler, Toby, and Art Young, eds. 1990. *Programs That Work: Models and Methods for Writing Across the Curriculum.* Portsmouth, N.H.: Heinemann, Boynton/Cook.

Gere, Anne Ruggles, ed. 1985. *Roots in the Sawdust: Writing to Learn Across the Disciplines.* Urbana, Ill.: National Council of Teachers of English.

Griffin, C. Williams, ed. 1982. *Teaching Writing in All Disciplines.* San Francisco: Jossey-Bass.

Maimon, Elaine, Gerald Belcher, Gail Hearn, Barbara Nodine, and Finbarr O'Connor. 1981. *Writing in the Arts and Sciences.* Cambridge, Mass.: Winthrop.

Martin, Nancy, ed. 1983. *Writing Across the Curriculum Pamphlets: A Selection from the Schools Council and London University Institute of Education Joint Project: Writing Across the Curriculum.* Upper Montclair, N.J.: Boynton/Cook.

Martin, Nancy, Pat D'Arcy, Bryan Newton, and Robert Parker. 1976. *Writing and Learning Across the Curriculum, 11–16.* London: Schools Council Publications.

Russell, David. 1991. *Writing in the Academic Disciplines, 1870–1990: A Curricular History.* Carbondale: Southern Illinois Univ. Press.

Steffens, Henry, and Mary Jane Dickerson. 1987. *Writer's Guide: History.* Lexington, Mass.: D. C. Heath.

Tchudi, Stephen, and Joanne Yates. 1983. *Teaching Writing in the Content Areas: Senior High School.* Washington, D.C.: National Education Association.

Walvoord, Barbara, and E. Fassler. 1982. *Helping Students Write Well: A Guide for Teachers in All Disciplines.* New York: MLA.

Young, Art, and Toby Fulwiler, eds. 1986. *Writing Across the Disciplines: Research Into Practice.* Upper Montclair, N.J.

9

Using Videotape to Enhance Instruction

ROBERT VAN GULICK AND MICHAEL LYNCH

During the past decade videotape technology has been used widely and successfully at Syracuse University to provide both faculty members and graduate teaching assistants with valuable feedback on their teaching. Neither of us claims to have any official or professional expertise regarding video technology; we are not theorists of its pedagogical use nor have we done any scientific studies of its value. But as a result of our experience at Syracuse, we do have considerable informal knowledge that commends videotaping as a worthwhile improvement exercise.

Why Videotape?

If you have not used videotaping to evaluate teaching the technique might strike you as just a gimmick, a bit of trendy electronic gadgetry with little real educational value. In our experience, that has not been the typical reaction, at least not a publicly voiced one. Though videotaping is not a miracle tool, nor an all-purpose substitute for other methods of evaluating teaching, it does have unique advantages.

• Videotaping is a great motivator and generates considerable interest. Although we live in a video-saturated age, we are not all that accustomed to watching ourselves perform, especially in the lead role. We cannot help but become immediately engaged and actively involved in the process. The video-based section of our own TA orientation program, for example, regularly generates the most interest from the participants.

• Videotaping provides a concrete focus for discussion. While discussions of general principles and theoretical abstractions can sometimes be of help in our efforts to improve our teaching, they frequently fail to make real contact with our actual practice. Videotapes of our teaching in our classrooms do provide such discussions with a real-life, concrete, focus. Our strengths and weaknesses, as well as our style and technique of delivery, are readily accessible for analysis. The likelihood that our teaching will improve also increases because discussion can focus on our specific context, approach, and problems. Suggestions for change can be tailor-made for each unique situation.

• Videotaping provides a powerful means to reverse perspective. What other technique allows us to observe our own performance in the classroom? One goal of videotaping is to make instructors more self-aware and reflective as they teach. Even senior and accomplished instructors have been greatly surprised by aspects of their teaching that were first revealed to them as they watched themselves on videotape.

• Videotaping produces a record that can be reviewed and reexamined over time. We can view a particular aspect of our teaching several times, either in the course of a single session or in multiple sessions on different dates. In this way, we can gauge how our teaching changes and determine what results those changes have produced.

• Videotaping gives us a relatively unobtrusive window into the classrooms of our fellow instructors. Most instructors rarely if ever observe their peers' teaching. This is unfortunate because it deprives everyone involved of valuable opportunities to learn from one another. Videotaping helps break down reluctance to cross the threshold of another's classroom; it takes us perceptually inside without having to go there bodily. In fact, most instructors find the look into another's classroom both fascinating and useful. And indeed, having once crossed the threshold electronically, instructors tend to be much more comfortable about attending in person.

To use videotape effectively requires attention to two sorts of "how-to" questions—logistical and technical. These include questions about how to make quality tapes, and questions about how to view and critique those tapes once they have been made.

Making Videotapes

Most colleges and universities have in-house video support services that can supply equipment and trained personnel (often work-study students) to videotape a class at a very modest cost. While such centralization of services is an appropriate way to introduce a campus to videotaping, it is less than ideal once the technique has become more widely used. At that point, a more readily available supply of equipment and trained operators is desirable, for example, for an academic department to have its own video set-up that can be used to tape and view the teaching of the instructors within the department. Teaching assistants can be trained to use a video camera and called upon to tape one another's classes, thus providing a large, continuously renewing pool of skilled operators. An easy step-by-step instruction sheet can be written so that each new generation of teaching assistants can be quickly trained. One important benefit is that the teaching assistants actively engage with the ongoing improvement of their teaching from the outset and make regular visits to one another's classrooms to do the videotaping—another way to overcome the "don't cross the threshold" problem.

Two recurrent problems of technique are worth anticipating and correcting early. The first concerns camera angle: if at all possible place the camera in the room such that it covers both the instructor and the students. It is very helpful to have the students on the tape, even if they appear only occasionally or only when they are speaking. The second concerns audio recording: picking up good sound in a classroom will be difficult if you use only the in-camera microphone. Adding a supplementary multidirectional microphone, placed to pick up both instructor and students, is desirable.

Using the Videotapes

Microteaching

During the orientation program at Syracuse University, each new teaching assistant makes a five-minute prepared presentation, relevant to his or her discipline, to a small group of peers. The group leader, an experienced teaching assistant, videotapes the presentation. At a later session the presentations are critiqued by the same small group in a friendly and constructive manner. The group watches the tapes in succession, following each with a ten to fifteen minute evaluation. The presenter is always invited to comment first, which helps reduce anxiety because it gives that teaching assistant the opportunity to preemptively note any obvious weaknesses in his or her performance. Then the other members of the group are invited to comment; the group leader takes the role of facilitator rather than that of an authority figure.

The leader's role is to encourage the new teaching assistants to become constructive critics rather than to act as the primary evaluators of the videotapes. In that role, the leader encourages the group to try to come up with concrete suggestions for dealing with any problems noted in the taped performance. For example, rather than merely noting that the teaching assistant speaks too quickly or does not allow enough time for questions, the group tries to suggest specific solutions such as silently counting to ten after inviting a question. Ideally, the group develops a cooperative problem-solving spirit. Finally, the leader focuses on just one or two key aspects of the teaching assistant's teaching and offers one or two concrete suggestions for improvement. The goal is to make the evaluation summary sufficiently focused that the teaching assistant will be able to carry over the suggestions to his or her subsequent teaching.

In general, when evaluating tapes it is easiest to focus on the obvious features of the presentation, such as how well the instructor's voice projects or how well he or she conveys enthusiasm or maintains eye contact with the audience. But it is both possible and desirable to expand the discussion to include other less-apparent features, such as the clarity or organization of the presentation. The table below is a helpful list of criteria drawn up by the teaching fellows at Syracuse University for use in the video segment of the TA Orientation Program.

Using Video to Improve Instruction
Sample Criteria for Providing Feedback

I. **Oral Presentation**
    A. Voice Inflection/modulation
    B. Speed of presentation/pacing
    C. Appropriate use of pauses
    D. Loudness of voice
    E. Articulation

II. Techniques to Maintain Interest
   A. Makes appropriate gestures and body movements
   B. Maintains eye contact
   C. Speaks directly to audience/involves students
   D. Moves around room appropriately/narrows actual physical distance between the speaker and audience
   E. Conveys enthusiasm, energy, and confidence

III. Organization and Preparation
   A. Logical order of information
   B. Clarity of major points
   C. Appropriate use of examples
   D. Evidence of preparation, such as not constantly looking at notes
   E. Evidence of clear learning objectives and lesson purpose
   F. Vocabulary appropriate for audience
   G. Right amount of material

IV. Attention to Students
   A. Understands skills and background of class members
   B. Shows genuine concern for students
   C. Uses humor appropriately
   D. Uses good classroom questioning techniques
   E. Evokes classroom discussion effectively

V. Use of Media
   A. Uses media appropriately as a teaching tool
   B. Legible/right size
   C. Diagrams/problems labeled
   D. Uses media in an orderly way/evidence of organization
   E. Demonstrates the effective use of media in the classroom

Microteaching during new teaching assistant orientation has three main goals:

• To reduce some of the anxiety that new teaching assistants typically have about going into the classroom. A positive experience, with useful and balanced feedback from their peers (as well as the experience of watching their peers go through the same exercise), helps them feel more confident and comfortable with their new teaching role. This is especially true for international teaching assistants, who often have additional concerns about the cultural transition they are making. It is very important that the tone of the evaluation sessions is positive and constructive.

• To provide each new teaching assistant with one or two concrete suggestions for improving his or her teaching. The net improvement may be small, but it should make a difference and will be the
first step of an ongoing self-improvement process.

• To make the new teaching assistants more self-aware observers
and constructive critics of their own teaching and that of their peers.
The orientation is intended as just the first step in a long process of
cooperative and self-critical evaluation aimed at continuous development and improvement as teachers.

Videotaping Throughout the Semester

The Syracuse University philosophy department uses videotaping throughout the semester to improve teaching and encourage reflection. Every professor is encouraged, and every teaching assistant
and graduate instructor is required, to videotape his or her class at
least once a semester. Because new instructors in particular benefit
considerably from seeing themselves teach, they participate in special
evaluation sessions and often have themselves videotaped more than
once a term.

To facilitate scheduling, the department has set up a buddy system: instructors who will be using the video equipment pair up with
someone else who has a compatible schedule. This way, the members
of the pair can videotape each other, working with someone with
whom they feel comfortable. All new teaching assistants must be videotaped by the fourth week of classes; all others must be videotaped
by the sixth week. The reason for this is simple: the longer the instructors wait, the less time they have to incorporate into their classes
what they learn from the videotaping process.

Videotapes are used in several different settings. Perhaps the
most important, and certainly the easiest to arrange, is for the instructor to view and critique his or her own videotape alone. In the case of
beginning instructors, especially those who are teaching an entire
course by themselves for the first time, a group feedback session is
often more useful. Such a session typically includes all the new teaching assistants, along with a more senior graduate student teacher and
an experienced faculty member. Each of the new instructors brings a
copy of his or her videotape, rewound to a suitable five-to ten-minute
segment. After each tape is shown, discussion begins with that instructor describing what he or she did and did not like about the segment.
Starting with a self-critique emphasizes the constructive rather than

destructive nature of the enterprise and makes everyone more comfortable. Next, the other participants offer both encouragement and suggestions on how to overcome certain problems. Again, the emphasis should be on constructive criticism; empty compliments and purely negative commentary are both discouraged.

Classroom Videotaping for Faculty Members

Teaching-improvement program workshops for faculty can focus on the use of videotaping. Each participant brings to the workshop a videotape that he or she has made of a class he or she teaches. The workshops will probably include some general discussions about classroom issues, but the main focus is the tapes. Each participant shows a segment about fifteen to twenty minutes long which is followed by an evaluation session much like that described above. The workshops produce a wealth of valuable information and technique. They help to build a subculture of faculty members from different departments who share a commitment to the importance of teaching and its ongoing development. Videotape techniques can benefit experienced and accomplished senior instructors just as they do new instructors who are beginning their careers.

These preceding examples are just three of the many ways in which videotaping can be used to improve instruction. Other ways are surely possible. Videotaping is not a substitute for all other forms of evaluation; in particular, it should not completely replace having someone visit the class and later provide the instructor with feedback. Only through in-person visits can an evaluator get a true sense of the classroom dynamics and student involvement. Nonetheless, videotaping has some unique advantages of its own, and an ideal program for improving teaching will include both videotaping and in-person visits.

10

Motivating Students

RUTH V. SMALL AND R. DAVID LANKES

"I was never sure I had a chance for success."
"The vocabulary was way over my head."
"Class sessions seemed unprepared and disorganized."
"Expectations were vague and inconsistent."
"I never got any positive feedback."
"The lectures were boring and monotonous."
"There were no real-life applications."
"There was never any interaction."
"I didn't feel challenged."

These comments are typical of the responses highly motivated graduate student teaching assistants at Syracuse University offered when asked to reflect on some of their past educational experiences.[1] Although these students were intrinsically motivated enough to persevere in the pursuit of their educational goals, there are many others whose experiences have had such a negative impact on them that they alter their educational aspirations or, worse, drop out altogether.

In this chapter, we present an organized structure and a selection of instructional strategies for motivating student learning. We begin by defining motivation as it has typically been described in the psychology and education literature and then briefly present two current

1. All student quotations appearing in this chapter were collected as data in a research study on what motivates student learning conducted by Ruth V. Small, assistant professor, Syracuse University, and Bernie Dodge, professor, San Diego State University.

models for designing motivating instruction. We conclude with an integrated framework for designing motivating instruction which synthesizes those models and identifies a variety of complementary strategies for motivating students to learn.

Defining Motivation

How do you know when your students are motivated? Some think that certain physical signs such as eye contact, smiles, and head nods, are evidence of student motivation. For others it is behaviors such as asking questions and participating in class. Still others measure student motivation by the quality and/or quantity of student work.

Research on human motivation acknowledges these and other behaviors as manifestations of a broader measure of motivation—effort (Porter and Lawler 1968). Furthermore, effort mandates the presence of two major prerequisites: value (i.e., students must value the learning task, considering it to be of personal worth, interesting, useful, and important to them) and expectation to succeed (i.e., students believe they are capable of successfully learning or performing the learning task). Both prerequisites must be present for students to put forth effort and be motivated. Instructors can directly maintain or increase student motivation by maximizing students' expectations for success and by increasing the perceived value of the learning task. As an instructor, you can have an impact on both of these prerequisites through thoughtful and systematic instructional planning.

Although most of the research on motivation has been conducted in the context of the workplace (i.e., what motivates workers to produce more and faster), in recent years some educational theorists have turned their attention to the classroom, exploring what factors influence a student's desire to learn (e.g., Keller 1983; Wlodkowski 1991). A good instructor strives to provide students with what researchers call a "flow" experience; that is, one in which students become so captivated by the learning experience that they become totally immersed in it, to the point of losing self-awareness (Csikszentmihalyi 1975; 1978). As students emerge from this stimulating and fulfilling experience, they may feel a sense of time and space disorientation while feeling exhilarated.

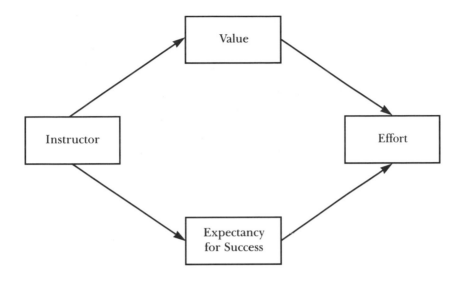

Models for Designing Motivating Instruction

In the quest to design and facilitate motivating learning experiences, two models have currently emerged. In the first, Wlodkowski (1991) views learning motivation as responding to student needs along a time continuum. His Time Continuum Model specifies that students enter the learning experience with certain attitudes and needs about learning in general as well as learning in the specific context. Once students become involved in the learning process, they seek continuing stimulation and emotional experiences in order to remain motivated. As they conclude the learning process, students expect to attain competence and receive reinforcement. Wlodkowski's model provides a descriptive framework for organizing motivating instruction.

Another recently developed motivation model provides a structure for including motivating instructional strategies throughout the learning episode. The ARCS Model of Motivational Design, developed by Keller, is largely based on expectancy-value theory. The ARCS Model identifies four major motivational factors (*A*ttention, *R*elevance, *C*onfidence, *S*atisfaction), all of which must be considered when planning an instructional event. The degree to which each factor must be addressed depends on the needs, interests, and abilities of the students; the difficulty and complexity of the subject matter; the level of learning objectives; and the constraints of the learning environment. Keller's model provides a prescriptive framework for selecting appropriate instructional strategies to motivate student learning (e.g., Keller 1983; 1987). It consists of four major factors for consideration.

Attention

> I was sitting in class. . . . Though I know I needed to understand the material and to pay attention, I just could not. Every week I would sit in that class bored to sleepiness. The teacher would give incredibly boring, dry lectures—straight out of the readings. Hardly any other comments were given. Once in a blue moon he would write something cryptic on the board or use the overhead. By the end of the semester, weekly attendance was down to a hard core ten from about 16 originally.

The *Attention* factor is concerned with identifying techniques that capture student curiosity and interest early in the instruction and maintain that attention even beyond the end of the learning episode. Strategies must be incorporated that gain attention and sustain interest.

Relevance

> Last summer I was enrolled in an extension class. The class was supposed to teach me how to mainstream special education students into my regular classroom. The instructor . . . lectured for two weeks on the definition and implementation of behavior modification. I was joined in my agony by thirty other teachers—all satisfying a newly imposed state requirement. We never did learn anything practical concerning mainstreaming.

Providing a more meaningful instructional context helps students understand the importance of learning something. *Relevance* techniques help students link the instructional content and methods to their needs and interests. This fosters student involvement in the learning process. Strategies must be incorporated that demonstrate and maintain relevance.

Confidence

The class was supposed to be a Friday morning seminar class in elementary education in which students would participate in discussion of problems and issues directly related to student teaching . . . Roll was called precisely at 8 A.M. with tardy marks given to those not present (all students were in fifth year college work). The content of the class was a step-by-step demonstration of how to make a pocket chart. Students were required to follow each step and perform the task. Negative remarks were directed at individual students by the instructor if they did not have the right materials or if they did not follow the exact directions. I was told to do one procedure over because I had taken a short cut.

Creating a positive climate for learning helps students develop competence and self-confidence. Strategies must be incorporated that establish, increase, or reinforce confidence. With particularly difficult, complex, unfamiliar, and/or abstract content, students may lack *Confidence* in their ability to learn. Learning goals and expectations should be both challenging and attainable for students in the class.

Satisfaction

I was in an undergraduate class in Victorian poetry. . . . It was a strictly lecture course and the prof sat at a table with a typing stand propped before him, reading lecture notes from old, yellowed, curling sheets of note paper. The professor's monotone voice, lack of eye contact, lack of humor (made the course boring). The class diminished from 40+ to 13.

When students feel that they have achieved learning success due to their ability and effort, they are likely to experience learning *Satisfaction*. This often results in a desire to continue learning. Strategies must be incorporated that promote satisfaction.

We favor a design framework that integrates Wlodkowski's and Keller's motivation models; i.e., it recommends a range of potential instructional strategies for motivating student learning and places them within a time sequence. Although the list of strategies is not exhaustive, we believe it provides general guidelines that you can apply to course design; these strategies are equally applicable to the design of a single lesson. Which (and how many) motivational strategies to apply depends on what is most appropriate for your learning situation and your learners.

Beginning the Instruction

Gain Attention

Provide novelty or mystery. Students react to unpredictable, perplexing, or incongruous stimuli in their environment. Such stimuli create interest and stimulate curiosity. Try using novel approaches or personal material to capture students' attention (Keller 1987).

Generate high level inquiry and thought. Begin with a thought-provoking statement or question for students to consider during your instruction. It helps students create a structure for the information presented throughout the course.

Demonstrate Relevance

Show how learning is worthwhile. Students like to learn things that will offer them benefits or a real advantage (Wlodkowski 1991). As instructors, we clearly recognize the importance of what we teach, but many of our students do not. Furthermore, although some learning tasks are intrinsically motivating, most people (even adults) seek out learning experiences in which the knowledge of skills to be learned has a personal utility to the learner (Zemke and Zemke 1981). Describing the usefulness and/or importance of the learning task requires that you understand your learners' world.

Relate new content to previous or future learning. Make learning more relevant by helping students understand the importance of the content or skills to be learned in the context of what they already have learned and what still needs to be learned. Specify the relevance in the first class session.

Design and, when necessary, revise learning objectives to be compatible with student needs, values, and abilities. Determine early where your students are in the learning process and where they expect to be at the end of this course. One technique is to administer a student questionnaire in the first class session that collects information about each student, including why they are taking your course and what they expect to learn. This technique also allows you to quickly correct any incorrect assumptions about what the course will be like and/or adjust the course to meet student expectations.

Establish Confidence

Set moderately challenging, attainable learning objectives. If instruction is too easy, students get bored; if it is too difficult, students become anxious. Most students prefer instruction that presents at least a moderate, "just within reach" learning challenge (Wlodkowski 1991).

Specify learning requirements as clearly and thoroughly as possible. Describe the scope of content to be learned and clearly articulate your learning expectations on the first day of class. Reinforce them by providing students with a comprehensive course syllabus that includes learning goals and expectations, scope of content, and criteria for evaluation. Further clarify assignments and criteria for success by showing students exemplary models of assignments or projects completed in the past by students like themselves. "Seeing similar others perform successfully can raise efficacy expectations in observers who then judge that they too possess the capabilities to master comparable activities. . . . Modeling displays convey information about the nature and predictability of environmental events" (Bandura 1982, 126–27).

Set mutually determined learning goals. Set an appropriate difficulty level that is compatible with students' abilities and prior knowledge or experience. Where possible, help set the learning goals and criteria for evaluation.

During the Instruction

Sustain Interest

Direct students' attention to important content. Use cueing statements (e.g., "This is particularly important"; "Pay close attention here") to alert students that the information you are about to present is important for learning success.

Vary presentation methods, media, and materials. People tend to pay more attention to things that are changing than to things that are static (Wlodkowski 1991). Combining lectures with other presentation methods such as participatory activities and visual aids creates higher levels of interest.

Use memory enhancement techniques. Techniques such as mnemonics, visual representations, and personal anecdotes may help students remember important factual content.

Encourage active student participation and active learning. "Tell me, I forget. Show me, I remember. Involve me, I understand." *Ancient Proverb.*

Most students prefer activities that allow them to interact and be actively involved in their learning (Brophy 1987). Techniques that increase learner participation will result in increased learner effort, ownership, and achievement (Young 1982). Build into each class session some type of activity that requires students to participate, such as small-group discussion, brainstorming, simulation exercises, lab experiences, debate, problem-solving case studies, or role-playing exercises.

Foster ongoing inquiry. Encourage students to ask questions during each class session. This allows you to clarify content that is not well understood, correct misconceptions, and elaborate on points of interest.

Use humor where appropriate. When used spontaneously or deliberately, through such strategies as humorous anecdotes or cartoons, humor can calm learning anxiety and establish a friendlier, more comfortable learning environment.

Maintain Relevance

Relate content to familiar, real-world experiences. Allow students to draw on their own knowledge and experiences and relate them to the content you are teaching. Also bring in practitioners working in the field or students who have previously taken the course to provide testimonials about its usefulness and importance.

Model desired behaviors. In a review of the research, Sherman et al. (1987) found certain behaviors to be indicators of teaching excellence at the college level. These include knowledge (of subject matter and of effective teaching methods), enthusiasm (for subject matter and for teaching it to others), clarity, stimulating interest and thinking, preparation and organization.

Allow opportunities to apply learning. Provide knowledge or skill-building practice exercises or sessions such as labs and projects that allow students to use what they are learning as they are learning it.

Increase Confidence

Describe unfamiliar or difficult concepts in more concrete ways. When teaching new, unfamiliar, difficult, or abstract content, you will often need to give students more than one explanation. It is useful to prepare alternative, preferably visual, explanations (e.g., a flow chart, a video, a drawing). Always define and explain new terms, preferably both orally and in writing (e.g., glossary of new terms). In addition, you could use examples, anecdotes, analogies, case studies, and metaphors to clarify content. Provide additional examples when content is particularly difficult or abstract.

Progress from easier, more familiar, basic content to more complex, abstract, and /or difficult content. If teaching a basic or introductory course, begin with what the students already know and progress to increasingly more difficult concepts and/or skills, building in periodic reviews. If you are teaching an advanced course, begin with a review of the more basic known information and build on that knowledge as the content becomes more difficult.

Allow thinking and reflecting time. When asking questions in class, provide time for students to think before responding. Research has shown that teachers often do not allow their students enough time after the question is asked to retrieve what they know from their long-term memory. As instructors, we tend to be uncomfortable at first with silence and will reflexively either call on a student or answer the question ourselves. Rowe (1987) found that by allowing just three to five seconds after posing a question, instructors got more students to respond and to offer better responses.

Assess learning at various points during the instruction. Evaluating student learning throughout the instruction allows you to identify what learning has occurred and where you need to revise or modify learning goals, instructional methods, and/or content. Continuous assessment throughout a course could include techniques such as quizzes, oral questions, application exercises, and short-term projects.

Provide timely, and regular, informational feedback on learning progress. Students need to know what and how well they are learning, and where and how they can improve. Follow up the learning assessment described above with prompt written and/or verbal feedback that relates to your evaluation criteria. In addition, make yourself regularly available for consultation and learning guidance through regularly scheduled office hours, or by being available before or after class.

Allow students some control over their own learning. Give students opportunities to make choices about their own learning (Keller 1987). For example, they can choose topics and formats for assignments and projects or how and when to be evaluated (Wlodkowski 1991).

Provide sincere praise for learning effort. Praise can be highly effective motivation throughout the learning activity, but only when it is sincere and emphasizes the link between effort and learning success.

When tied to competence and achievement of challenging tasks, it can boost the student's self-esteem (Dweck 1986). Wlodkowski (1991) uses a "3S-3P" mnemonic (Sincere, Specific, Sufficient; Properly attributed, Praiseworthy, Preferred) to guide the use of praise as a reward: "Praise (and other rewards) should be Sincere, Specific, Sufficient, and Properly attributed for genuinely Praiseworthy behavior in a manner Preferred by the learner" (232).

Concluding the Instruction

Reinforce Confidence

Help students set new learning goals. When students are motivated and excel, they often want to continue their learning as a natural consequence of learning success. You can encourage and support their desire for more learning. An instructor can recognize a student's learning competence and recommend him or her for advanced or honors courses in the same content area or provide reading lists and other independent learning options.

Promote Satisfaction

Use fair and consistent learning assessment methods. All of your tests and other learning assessment methods should be consistent with your learning objectives and the content presented. Tests reflect not only student learning but also the effectiveness of the instruction.

Reward learning achievement. Reinforce connections between achievement and effort by giving praise and other tangible or symbolic rewards (e.g., grades, certificates) at the completion of a learning sequence. Acknowledge exemplary work by displaying student work or asking students to make presentations.

Allow students to use or apply their newly gained knowledge or skills. Arrange internship or practicum experiences in which students may apply what they have learned in the classroom to a real-world setting.

In this chapter, we defined motivation in terms of expectancy-value theory, described two current educational models of motivation, and presented an integrated framework for those models with a selection of strategies for motivating student learning. Throughout the chapter we have ourselves used a number of motivational strategies to gain and sustain your attention, demonstrate and maintain the

MOTIVATIONAL FACTORS

TIME SEQUENCE	Attention	Relevance	Confidence	Satisfaction
Beginning	**Gain attention.** • Introduce novelty/mystery • Generate high level inquiry/thought	**Demonstrate relevance.** • Show learning is worthwhile • Relate new content to previous/future learning • Design/revise goals	**Establish confidence.** • Set moderately challenging, attainable goals • Specify learning requirements • Set mutually determined goals	
During	**Sustain attention.** • Direct attention to important content • Vary methods, media, materials • Use memory enhancement techniques • Encourage participation/active learning • Foster ongoing inquiry • Use humor	**Maintain relevance.** • Relate to real-world • Model desired behaviors • Allow opportunities to apply learning	**Increase confidence.** • Describe unfamiliar/difficult concepts in concrete ways • Progress from basic to more complex content • Allow thinking/reflecting time • Assess learning at various points • Provide timely/regular feedback • Allow learning control • Provide sincere praise	
Concluding			**Reinforce confidence.** • Set new goals	**Promote satisfaction.** • Use fair/consistent assessment methods • Reward achievement • Provide opportunities to use/apply new knowledge/skills

relevance of the information presented; to establish, increase, and reinforce your confidence; and to promote your satisfaction that you can take many of these strategies and apply them to your own instruction. The framework (summarized in the figure on previous page) provides you with an organized, systematic instructional planning tool that considers the importance of both motivating students' desire to learn and achieving learning goals. We also provide you with a list of related readings for those interested in continuing to learn about this topic.

Designing motivating instruction can result in successful learning episodes where students feel accomplished and inspired.

> I can't quite remember the situation, at least not for the whole presentation. There were about thirty students present, one instructor and one guest. Most of the class content was lecture. The instructor used the overhead projector extensively and threw out a lot of stimulating questions for student response and reaction. Whether or not it was used in this particular session I can't recall, but the instructor had a tremendous knack of drawing quiet students into the learning. I had a great feeling of being part of a learning environment.

11

Gender, Race, and Ethnicity in the Classroom

JUDY LONG, WYNETTA DEVORE, AND IAN LAPP

All of us who are involved in academia—students, teachers, administrators and staff—embody personal biographies and group identities that reflect class, sex, race, ethnicity and sexuality. The groups that have shaped us constitute "invisible colleges"[1] (Crane 1972) that surround us as we work. These are part of the learning environment just as much as are classrooms and textbooks. Our invisible colleges filter our assumptions about intellectual ancestry and posterity, and influence the ease or difficulty with which we place ourselves in the intellectual tradition of our field.

Often, the teaching staff of the university fails to reflect the diversity of the population, presenting an unnecessarily limited image of higher education. When we ignore diversity, we can create obstacles for students who do not match or fit the sex, race, age, ethnicity, or sexual orientation of the "generic professor." Groups that are ignored in our teaching, research, and writing become blind spots in our theories, lacunae in the knowledge base of our disciplines. They become ghosts at the feast that can haunt the teaching and learning process.

A protocol of impersonality that renders these identities "invisible" and unmentionable may compromise our teaching mission. In minimizing our personal and group identities we deny diversity. For beneath academia's surface of seeming continuity and homogeneity lies a substratum of diversity. Connecting with the invisible colleges—

1. We are adopting Diana Crane's phrase here, and using it to refer to the significant groups of which each of us is a part.

our own and those of our students—is one way of approaching the inclusive classroom. In this chapter we seek to reverse the invisibility of race, class, sex, and ethnicity and explore the advantages to be gained from an educational process that recognizes and capitalizes upon our diversity. We will be thinking concretely in terms of an inclusive classroom that allows students, teaching assistants, and professors to learn from one another in a safe and uninhibited environment enriched by diversity.

Demographics and Trends in College Classrooms of the Present and Future

In our classrooms, the group looking back at us is considerably more diverse than the faculty they see before them. Population projections indicate that the student body (like the population as a whole) will become more different from the faculty in the twenty-first century than it is today. The traditional pool that supplies scientific and technology-oriented workers is shrinking; we will need to turn to women and minorities who have been historically absent from these fields (Oakes 1990). Ethnic and racial diversity is increasing substantially in the society at large; it is estimated that soon after the turn of the century 42 percent of the secondary school pool will be composed of minority students. Yet research shows that African-American, Latino, and Asian faculty are rare. Production of African-American and Latino Ph.D.'s has decreased in recent years, pointing to an even greater scarcity in future than at present (Garza 1993).

Campuses continue to be segregated by race and sex. Top administration in higher education is typically white and male, with an occasional token minority or female individual.[2] Faculty ranks are

2. Gender, race, and class are institutionalized in the staffing patterns and traditions of the university. White males come to personify leadership, which can create particular problems for women, international students, and members of racial minorities. Cultural expectations for women and minorities may be at variance with the prerogatives of the professorial role. A kind of "statistical prejudice" can make students resistive. Thus nonwhite or nonmale teachers sometimes encounter racist and sexist behavior from students. Current research reveals that women college teachers must contend with direct challenges to their professional authority. The introduction of inappropriate sexist behavior (such as obscene language or drawings) into the classroom has become a prevalent problem for women teachers. Women of color are subject to racist harassment as well. These harassment hazards have become so widespread that instructors are required to devise counterstrategies (Sandler 1989). It should be noted, however, that harassment of this sort is a collective problem not an individual one. It must be addressed at the departmental and university level.

dominated at the top by men, in the lower ranks by women. On any particular campus, there may be a number of departments with no women faculty. Racial and ethnic minorities, on many campuses, are virtually invisible. Moreover, the past quarter-century has seen very little change in these ratios. Meanwhile, the sex composition of the student pool is changing considerably faster. In some professional schools, women students are approaching parity with men. The percentage of female graduate students has been steadily increasing in many doctoral programs. Women are the majority in the student bodies of many undergraduate institutions. Demographic data continue to show an underrepresentation of African-American and Latino undergraduates in mathematics and the natural sciences and an overrepresentation in disciplines leading to low income jobs (education, the humanities, and the social sciences). For African-American and Latino women this imbalance is magnified by the additional forces of sex role stereotyping.

This is no dry statistical message; the mismatch between faculty and student profiles has implications for classroom dynamics, for attrition and retention, for the fields and futures that students choose and fail to choose. For many faculty members, the increasing diversity of the student body brings unprecedented challenges. In dealing effectively with these, we will need to become more aware of ourselves and more aware of classroom dynamics. This may require the development of pedagogical principles that are more reflexive, and a classroom style that incorporates process. If our professional training has focused on content to the exclusion of these other factors, many of us will need to explore issues of pedagogy seriously for the first time. Valuable resources are to be found in new research on classroom responses of speech or silence, on the relationship between teaching and learning, and on development of an inclusive curriculum.[3]

Presiding Over the Inclusive Classroom: Activities for Professors

The teacher, whether tenured professor or graduate assistant, has control over many aspects of teaching: not only content but style; not only lectures but nonverbal messages; materials, exercises and evaluation; and of course classroom dynamics, process, and feedback. Each of these can affect student learning and, in the longer run, students' persistence, aspiration setting, and retention. Moving effec-

3. See, for example, the work of Schoem, Frankel, Zuniga, and Lewis (1993).

tively toward the inclusive classroom means shaping our self-presentation and the group dynamics of our classrooms in such a way as to increase commitment and reduce alienation.

Embodying and Enacting the Teacher Role. In thinking about diversity a good place to begin is with ourselves. We know that, in entering the classroom as teachers, we incorporate attributes of sex, race, and ethnicity. Those who see and hear us impute additional identities of sexuality and social class. Before we have spoken a word, we have set in motion a dynamic that involves the invisible colleges of our students. When you walk into the classroom, do your students see a teacher or an African-American teacher? A professor or a woman professor? In the classroom our personal attributes are undeniably visible to our students. Their responses to us reflect identities and histories of groups to which they and we belong.

Membership in our own invisible colleges shapes our teaching style, the jokes and anecdotes we employ, the way we address our students, the way we solicit and evaluate their participation. In our classroom behavior, we can inadvertently give offense by disregarding diversity, and undermine our intellectual purpose by introducing divisiveness. Jokes that might pass without comment in some social settings are deeply offensive to certain groups and can have a shocking effect in the classroom context. Again, by virtue of being born into certain groups, we have been exposed to stereotypes of other groups. Giving expression to such unexamined stereotypes in our professional role may undermine our fundamental goals as teachers. For example, the way we express expectations for the achievement of males vs. females, of blacks vs. whites, may create obstacles to that very achievement. Unconscious behaviors on our part can create a "chilly classroom climate" or even constitute a "hostile environment" for women, for lesbians and gay men, for members of racial and ethnic minorities. Nonverbal elements of our classroom behavior also send a message. Classroom studies have revealed that boys get more attention from teachers than do girls, even in elementary schools (where women teachers predominate). In the university, where male teachers predominate, sex differentials in attention and teacher expectations are marked. The encounter between the invisible colleges we represent and those represented by our students is one place where greater self-consciousness of teachers can contribute to a more inclusive classroom climate.

Teachers who are conscientious about avoiding racial and sexual stereotypes may still give offense by selecting examples that assume that all students are involved in heterosexual dating; this renders gay, lesbian, and bisexual students invisible and their lives illegitimate. Even when we are scrupulous to avoid homophobic references in the classroom, bias may creep into informal settings. In socializing with our peers outside the classroom, we may exclude gay and lesbian colleagues by assuming, for example, that marriage is in everyone's future.

For our students, we do more than embody our social and ethnic identities; their images of us are constitutive of the academic profession itself, and the scholarly disciplines we practice. We represent not only ourselves but also our fields. Students' response to us shapes their image of the course content and the discipline. One way we can increase diversity is through the materials we select and the way we deal with them in the classroom. Where the established paradigms or canon of our disciplines neglect the contributions of diverse cultural traditions, we can expect to be challenged by our students. As teachers we must fulfill the obligations to the past and to the future. We must not reproduce the blind spots in our own training and deny diversity. We have much to gain by extending the knowledge base beyond our personal reach and the narrowness of the disciplinary tradition. Our commitment to completeness and validity underscores a concern for diversity. Diversity needs to be a consideration in the selection and presentation of content, in texts, in formulating the research agenda as well as in the face-to-face world of the classroom.

Selecting materials. Acknowledging the power that we have as professors and graduate teaching assistants to select the texts and materials from which students learn, we must evaluate and redesign curricula. Our power to do so has significant potential for bridging or sustaining distance between invisible colleges. In the interests of scholarly thoroughness, we as teachers must continually seek out materials that will expand our knowledge.[4] Giving attention to diversity can lead us toward the materials that are needed. One way to tap into experiences different from our own is through the use of fiction and biography or autobiography. Although we as scholars rely on academic theorizing and its specialized literature, we know that they are foreign to most undergraduates and the ways in which they learn. Well-chosen novels or biographies can bridge the gap between these

---

4. Curriculum integration projects begun on many campuses twenty years ago have addressed these shortcomings, but in many institutions of higher education, much remains to be done today.

worlds, can expand diversity by symbolic means, and can help students learn to identify the societal and structural forces that shape the experiences of individuals. Meeting the students halfway requires the professor to select appropriate materials. Fiction can "give history a face," as in Toni Morrison's *Beloved* or Alice Walker's *The Color Purple*. The Civil Rights Movement in the south comes alive in Anne Moody's *Coming of Age in Mississippi*. Moody provides insights into race relations that could not be learned from other sources. Harry Edwards' *The Struggle That Must Be* (1980) reveals the experience of African-American students in white academia. Writers James Baldwin and J. California Cooper, James Alan McPherson and Douglas Ward Turner, Nikki Giovanni and Clarence Major provide other revelations about African-American people's experience in the United States. The neglect of gay and lesbian experience can be remedied through study of the works of Judy Grahn, Radclyffe Hall, Rita Mae Brown, Audre Lorde, Edmund White and Larry Duplechan. "Invisible colleges" materialize in the classroom when students read of the adolescent struggle with sexual identity in the context of race and class in Brown's *Rubyfruit Jungle* or Duplechan's *Blackbird*. From Paula Gunn Allen's *Spider Woman's Granddaughters*, students can learn the traditions of Native Americans, while Gloria Anzaldua's *Borderlands/La Frontera* provides a concrete instance of cultural duality.

Initially it may be a wrench for academics to teach materials that are "not really geography," for example, or "not scientific." This is not really such a radical departure, however. Most of our scholarly disciplines refer back, ultimately, to the "real world," and the problems we select often originate in this world. Following the traditions of our own disciplines, we create models, simulations, or fictions of this world in our laboratories, computers, seminars, or texts. Although materials that originate outside academia are initially unfamiliar, the tradeoff is appealing: in meeting our students halfway, we find that we are creating a more inclusive discourse. We find, too, that we can readily demonstrate how to think analytically and make use of concepts and techniques from our storehouse of disciplinary knowledge, using these materials. We could regard this as "naturalizing" theory.

Guiding group process in the classroom. As teachers we are responsible for the quality and atmosphere of our classrooms, whose dynamics provide models of intergroup relations, whether or not we guide the process with awareness. This is not mere happenstance: we must consciously shape the group climate of our classrooms. Teachers must model respectful and responsible classroom behavior. Class participation is desirable but may be disruptive; differences may surface and oppositions form around them. Some professors fear that recognizing diversity is the precursor of inescapable conflict and divisiveness. In today's climate of "hate speech" and "political correctness," discussing difference may seem like opening Pandora's box. We think, in contrast, that the classroom can be a place where "invisible colleges" enter into dialogue with one another. To be sure, this requires both learning and unlearning. The suggestions that follow concern techniques for eliciting, channeling, and strengthening communication in the classroom.

Groundrules. The teacher can establish groundrules that make offensive behavior unlikely. Many teachers find it desirable to establish norms for participation, for language, for listening respectfully, etc. Common elements in classroom groundrules emphasize learning to disagree with an argument without attacking a person; offering evidence instead of just assertions; learning to ask questions rather than make assertions; respect for differing opinions; and avoiding overgeneralization.

Classroom discussion. Sometimes professors have difficulty eliciting participation in class discussion. Some students seem to "have a lot to say" while others "have nothing to say." Current research reveals how wrong we can be to take this behavior at face value. The classroom often mirrors other settings where participation may be constrained (or facilitated) by one's sexual, racial, or class status. Silence may not indicate a lack of attention or interest. Both speech and silence may be motivated by factors other than the student's knowledge of the course content. Studies comparing women's and men's speech patterns consistently show that men speak more, interrupt more, and refer to each other more than to women. Other experiences may affect students' speech or silence. Students who have been victims of sexual assault, racial or sexual harassment, or child abuse can be wounded anew by cavalier or impersonal references that ignore the personal pain involved in such "social problems" (Konradi 1993). Silence sometimes signals the existence of these hidden injuries.

In some classrooms professors have no difficulty in getting students to talk, but they are concerned about the quality of discussion and the lack of critical thought. Initially you may notice that "discussion" in your class is peppered with the glib phrases of television talk show pundits. Some students who "have opinions" have no corresponding store of evidence. In order to modulate such patterns of participation, you may want to require that all students take a turn.

Taking turns and "equal time." You can facilitate turn-taking by organizing seats in a circle, where this is feasible. Introducing norms such as "equal time" will modify imbalances in participation. You can allot each student a specified amount of time—say, one minute or two—and regulate it with a pocket timer. As students take turns around the class, you can have the student whose turn is next hold and reset the timer. To eliminate interruptions, you may want to give the speaker a token when she or he takes the floor and have her or him turn it over to another student only after completing what she wants to say. These techniques are also effective in breaking up patterns that impede dialogue, such as the tendency of some students always to have the first word or the last word. If every student gets a turn (no one gets to "pass"), and you select a different student to begin each time, habits of listening and taking turns will develop.

One challenge for the inclusive classroom is to disarm the fear of difference. The most fundamental requirement is the cultivation of listening skills. In a class where students have learned listening skills, it is easier both to speak and to hear.

Listening skills. Almost always, students need practice in developing listening skills before they can accurately express someone else's position or engage in dialogue. Many students need to "think out loud" under conditions of respectful attention and active listening, before they can know what they think. Listening skills can readily be taught in the classroom. Students learn to work in pairs to give active, intelligent, appreciative attention to another, refraining from speech but communicating interest, empathy, and respect through nonverbal means such as eye contact, body posture, or nods. As they alternate speaking and listening, students become aware of the way another's active listening facilitates their own thinking. Being listened to awarely feels supportive and gives the individual more confidence in her thinking. The practice of taking turns creates "space" for less assertive students to participate on a par with more assertive ones. Active listening can be expanded to a group activity, where the speaker gets the advantage of attention from a number of others. Parity is maintained by taking turns around the circle, so that each person speaks. Teachers are often surprised at how thoughtful and powerful the discussion becomes when students are supported in this way.

The "speakout." Once listening skills are established and can be trusted, advanced forms of discussion and dialogue can be built upon this foundation. As a result of cultivating active listening, the inclusive classroom may provide an atmosphere of attentive respect in which members of different groups feel free to tell others what is hurtful about the stereotypes that target groups to which they belong. A valuable classroom technique is the "speakout," in which members of a group are invited to share personal experiences and "insider" information about what it is like growing up as a member of their community. Often it is useful for other members of the class to hear "what I never want to hear again:" epithets, questions, and comments that reveal the speaker's prejudice. These tend to be sufficiently concrete and colloquial that most members of the class can recognize their own or neighbors' prejudices in this everyday language. These "never again" phrases can initiate a discussion of the personal impact of group and intergroup prejudices. Recognizing that they participate in this everyday prejudice makes for a most educational collision with students' belief that they are not racist (sexist, homophobic). The speakout is particularly effective for communicating the experience of groups with which the students believe they have no contact—homosexuals, people with hidden disabilities, or working class people, for example.

Acquired listening skills can serve as the basis for expanding students' ability to learn about different groups. Once students have developed the skill of effective listening, individuals in the class will be more motivated to share experiences, to think out loud, to voice their legitimate curiosity about lives different from their own, to interrogate texts. The class is now far from its initial stereotyping, and ready to frame legitimate questions of generalization and typicality.

In addition to teaching listening skills and fostering participation, teachers interested in creating an inclusive classroom have employed a number of different techniques to increase the quality of analysis. Some of these techniques foster reflexivity by asking the student to reflect upon what she or he is reading and observing in the classroom, in the context of a privileged and private relationship with the teacher.[5]

Reaction cards. One means of opening a personal line of communication between the teacher and student is the regular use of "reaction cards." In a private contract between the two, the teacher can establish expectations and build habits that will ripen into analytic insight. The

---

5. We have long recognized that the intellectual insight consists of "making connections," but we have sometimes overlooked the importance of the human connection in making this happen. Belenky et al. (1986) observe that many people learn most readily in a context of interpersonal connection.

student can comment on the readings and issues, providing his own personal analysis. By this means a student who does not feel comfortable engaging in public discussion can cite the arguments found in the readings as well as offering his own opinions and ideas. As a way of engaging with ideas, this kind of private writing can prepare the student for dialogue rather than debate and establish the habit of disagreeing with ideas while avoiding personal attacks. This technique allows all students to voice their thoughts about the course as well as to bring up issues of diversity, classroom dynamics, or other topics. Both reaction cards and journals permit the silent student to have his or her say. This method of communication can be used to provide the teacher with feedback on questions that remain unanswered and issues requiring future attention.

Journals. Another technique that is widely used is having students keep a personal journal that records more extensive reactions to what they are reading, hearing, and viewing. In addition to making a record of their reading, students enter into a symbolic dialogue which includes their queries, dissents, and counterarguments. The teacher can guide the journal by questions that focus on gender, sexual orientation, race, ethnicity, age, class, and disability. Many courses emphasize journal keeping in a context of discovery. The journal can also have the function of rehearsal, making students more ready and eager to engage in discussion. By means of a journal a student can, for example, reflect on his experience with a minority faculty member —possibly his first—and receive a response that deepens his awareness of the dynamics of diversity. The private and respectful nature of this exchange bypasses the group dynamics that can silence some students in the classroom.

A valuable extension might be the "dialogue journal," where students identified with opposing positions write out their thoughts and feelings about the issues that divide them.[6] Such a journal can be a valuable part of students' dealing with difference. This writing can potentially serve as a preparation for a face-to-face exchange, which students may come to desire once they become convinced they understand the other's position and wish to explore common ground.

The "Dialogue with Society" journal is one in which the student engages symbolically with a larger element of society or with society itself. She or he may address questions to a particular ethnic group, for example, or to a historical period. This practice enhances the

6. We are indebted to Barbara Regenspan for this idea.

asking of telling questions and directs analytic attention to the supra-individual level.

Initially, students often fall into patterns of association and inter-action in the classroom that reflect the sex and race ratios prevailing there and in the larger society. These may set the initial terms for classroom participation; but if your goal is an inclusive classroom, you will need to change the rules. Teachers can use space and motion to trigger insight.

Exercises involving the use of space. Much can be done by using spatial aspects of the classroom to underscore issues of social catego-ries that connote separation or belongingness. One exercise that re-quires students to place themselves by means of a series of identifications is "The Line." Initially all students are on one side of the imaginary line that divides the room. As different categories are called out, students cross the line to the "minority" side of the room.[7] Physically committing themselves by this movement seems to enhance students' appreciation of how it feels to be "on the spot," subject to possibly embarrassing attention. By the end of the exercise, virtually all students have crossed the line, and the minority has become the majority. This exercise also demonstrates palpably that no one be-longs to a single category; in fact all of us have multiple identities. Other exercises that employ spatial classroom tasks include The Fish-bowl discussed in Schoem et al. (1993, 326–27) and the Take a Stand exercise.

Working in small groups. Many teachers make use of small groups to increase safety, provide attention, and create solidarity. The teacher can assign students to groups as a means of breaking up preexisting clusters. A teacher may want to break up initial groupings that are too homogeneous by assigning students to work in groups. Some professors begin the semester this way and allow individuals to move among groups, or create new groups after a period of time.

Student-guided research. Another powerful technique is the use of student-guided research. This approach can be effective in counter-acting certain initial attitudes, such as the perceived irrelevance of research and resistance to unwelcome facts about, for example, American society. In this technique students' own assumptions—in-cluding prejudices or stereotyped expectations—are translated into testable propositions which they investigate by exploring the research

7. Categories might include "women," "individuals under 18 years old," or "peo-ple who were raised Catholic."

literature. The process typically involves a confrontation between students' stereotypes and the empirical evidence. One payoff of student-guided research is that students "own" the information they acquire. They tend to tell others about it, and use it in discussions outside of class. An assignment that extends this payoff is asking students to apply, rather than merely report, what they have learned. Rather than following the format of the traditional academic research paper, you can pose a task where students must use their information to solve a problem. Such an assignment places students in a specified, concrete role where they must use and be responsible for knowledge. For example, students can be asked to assume the role of a family court judge who must write an opinion in a child custody dispute involving a lesbian parent. They must research the evidence on child outcomes in lesbian parenting situations and base their judgment upon it. The opinion they write is to serve as a guide to judges in other custody disputes. In another assignment, the student had the task, writing as the head of a middle school, of drafting a policy statement that spelled out procedures needed to support gay, lesbian, and bisexual students and their families in the vulnerable teenage years.

The importance of reflexivity and personal experience. In the inclusive classroom, the abstract categories of race, class, and gender come to life when students share their own experiences. The authors find that an amazing diversity in family structures is represented by students in the classrooms of our private, urban university. Students know more than we think they do (and more than they think they do) about ethnicity, gender, class, and sexuality. Learning about ethnicity, for example, can be personalized through students' recollections of holidays and family gatherings in which special foods and customs are recreated. Students can be asked to compile a family history, aided by the oldest family member available. By means of this assignment the individual discovers his family's place in the American social and political landscape, and there are collective benefits as well. The students hear about pride as well as oppression in the history of their own and other groups. Students who have little information about their heritage may find interviewing their own family members illuminating. Older relatives, in particular, can provide a context for practices that could seem disturbingly "different" or meaningless.

In teaching about gender, it is often effective to rely upon students' observational abilities and then refine these as students become able to "see" more elements of social structure. If they have opportunity to observe elementary-age children, in their families or in pre-school settings, for example, students can readily generate a set of observations about how children are treated, outfitted, praised, and mentored differently by sex. These observations can be linked to students' recollection of their early years—and soon, students have reproduced from their own experience the research finding that by age 4, children in U.S. society have learned very detailed maps of gender that specify occupations, attributes, and aspirations by sex. The social control functions of gender become visible for the first time.

Invisible Colleges as a Resource for Teaching and Learning

Taking diversity as the starting point allows scholars and teachers to go beyond the limitations of paradigms that claim to be "color-blind" or "universal." Our students of the future stand to benefit from a more complete exposure to diversity than we were afforded in the graduate training of the past. In the inclusive classroom, we preside over an extended discourse in which invisible colleges have a part, an expanded dialogue in which unaccustomed voices are heard. Each of the components we have discussed above—our embodied selves, the materials we choose, the way we model communication and interchange—contributes to the inclusive classroom. In addition, we can guide and develop classroom behavior in ways that increase and improve participation, understanding, and insight.

The inclusive classroom builds upon an idea of diversity as a richness of people who have different and common backgrounds, experiences, and points of view. An educational philosophy and prac-tice that celebrates diversity takes attentive, respectful, reciprocal lis-tening as the prototype of learning. This practice, faithfully followed, translates into a habit of mind that does not fear, despise, or attack difference. The inclusive classroom thus allows students, teaching assistants, and professors to learn from one another in a safe and uninhibited environment.

Our approach, emphasizing invisible colleges, supports avowing who we are in the classroom. Our own experiences underscore the insight that personal identity is composed of attributes of race, eth-nicity, sex, gender, and sexual orientation in combination. The invisi-ble colleges we embody should be woven into classroom discussions of these dimensions and their effects.

Recognizing multiplicity is a starting point.[8] From there we must move to an appreciation of complexity in diversity. While arguing that social groupings are significant for identity and understanding, we wish also to emphasize the heterogeneity subsumed by such social groups. Such groupings can be problematic if as a teacher you slip into assuming that a group such as male or Latino is monolithic or defined by essential attributes. The broad categories of gender, ethnicity, and sexuality contain great diversity. Some categories are manifestly artificial: Asian-Americans comprise many political histories, language groups, and cultures, as do Native-Americans and Latinos. All categories are subject to disputation, as identity is continually constructed and reconstructed. The inclusive classroom must leave room for this discourse of multiplexity to develop. We anticipate that pedagogical techniques such as those discussed in this chapter will facilitate the development of an open-ended inquiry that leads, not to fixed answers, but to ever more compelling questions.

Suggested Readings

The following are additional resources that address either specific or general issues of diversity.

Acuna, Rodolfo. 1972. *Occupied America: The Chicano's Struggle Toward Liberation*. San Francisco: Canfield Press.

Alba, Richard, ed. 1988. *Ethnicity and Race in the U.S.A.: Toward the Twenty-first Century*. New York: Routledge.

Albrecht, Lisa, and Rose Brewer, eds. 1990. *Bridges of Power: Women's Multicultural Alliances*. Philadelphia: New Society.

Anderson, Beverly J. 1990. "Minorities and Mathematics: The New Frontier and Challenge of the Nineties." *Journal of Negro Education* 59, no. 3:260–72.

Anderson, Margaret L., and Patricia Hill Collins. 1992. *Race, Class, and Gender: An Anthology*. Belmont, Calif.: Wadsworth.

Anderson, S. E. 1990. "Worldmath Curriculum: Fighting Eurocentrism in Mathematics." *Journal of Negro Education* 59, no. 3:348–59.

Anzaldua, Gloria. 1981. *This Bridge Called My Back: Writings by Radical Women of Color*. New York: Kitchen Table/Women of Color Press.

---

8. We recognize that no one identifies in terms of a single dimension. Indeed, the myth of a unitary identity may underlie the tendency to impose polar categories, and the related (and divisive) tendencies to hierarchize and to establish relations of centrality/peripherality.

Anzaldua, Gloria, ed. 1990. *Making Face, Making Soul-/Haciendo Caras: Creative and Critical Perspectives by Women of Color*. San Francisco: Aunt Lute Foundation Books.

Anzaldua, Gloria. 1987. *Borderlands/la Frontera*. San Francisco: Spinsters/Aunt Lute.

Atkinson, Donald R. 1991. The Mentorship of Ethnic Minorities in Professional Psychology. *Professional Psychol.* 22, no.4:336–38.

Baker, Gwendolyn C. 1983. *Planning and Organizing for Multicultural Instruction*. Reading, Mass.: Addison-Wesley.

Banks, James A., and C. A. Banks, eds. 1989. *Multicultural Education*. Boston: Allyn and Bacon.

Basow, Susan A. 1987. "Evaluations of College Professors: Effect of Professor's Sex-type and Sex and Student's Sex." *Psychology Reports*. 60, no. 2:671–78.

———. 1987. "Evaluations of College Professors: Effect of Professor's Sex-type and Sex and Student's Sex. *Psychology Reports* 60, no.2:671–78.

———. 1987. Student Evaluations of College Professors: Are Female and Male Professors Rated Differently? *Journal of Education Psychology* 79, no. 3:308–14.

Beam, Joseph. 1986. *In the Life: A Black Gay Anthology*. Boston: Alyson.

Belenky, Mary Field, Blythe McVicker, Clinchy, NancyRule Goldberger, and Jill Mattuck Tarule. 1986. *Women's Ways of Knowing*. New York: Basic Books.

Bernal, M. *Black Athena: The Afroasiatic Roots of Classical Civilization*. New Brunswick, N.J.: Rutgers Univ. Press.

Berryman, S. E. 1983. *Who Will Do Science?* New York: Rockefeller Foundation.

Bishop, Alan J. 1990. "Western Mathematics: The Secret Weapon of Cultural Imperialism." *Race and Class*. 32, no. 2:51–65.

Bohmer, Susanne, and Joyce L. Briggs. 1991. "Teaching Privileged Students About Gender, Race, and Class Oppression." *Teaching Sociology*. 19:154–63.

Branch, R. C., Y. Goodwin, and J. Gaulteri. "Making Classroom Instruction Culturally Pluralistic." *The Education Forum*.

Brant, Beth, ed. 1984. *A Gathering of Spirit: Writing and Art by North American Indian Women*. Montpelier, Vt: Sinister Wisdom.

Brown, Cherie. 1984. *The Art of Coalition-Building*. New York: American Jewish Committee.

Bruschke, Jon C. 1993. "Student Ethnocentrism, Dogmatism, and Evaluation: A Study of BAFA BAFA." *Simulation and Gaming* 24, no. 1:9–20.

Bunch, Charlotte, and Sandra Pollack, eds. 1983. *Learning Our Way: Essays in Feminist Education*. Trumansburg, N.Y.: Crossing Press.

Cannon, Lynn Weber. 1990. *Curriculum Transformation: Personal and Political*. Memphis, Tenn.: Memphis State Univ., Center for Research on Women.

Collins, P. H., and M. Anderson, eds. 1987. *Toward an Inclusive Sociology: Race, Class, and Gender in the Sociology Curriculum.* Washington D.C.: ASA.

Collins, Patricia Hill. 1986. "Learning from the Outsider Within: The Sociological Significance of Black Feminist Thought." *Social Problems* 33, no. 6:14–32.

Cornwell, Anita. 1983. *Black Lesbian in White America.* Tallahassee, Fla: Naiad Press.

Cotton, Anthony. 1989. "Anti-Racist Mathematics Teaching and the National Curriculum." *Mathematics Teaching.* 137:22–26.

Culley, M., and C. Portuges, eds. 1985. *Gendered Subjects: The Dynamics of Feminist Teaching.* Boston: Routledge and Kegan Paul.

Cummins, Jim. 1986. "Empowering Minority Students: A Framework for Intervention." *Harvard Educational Review.* 56 no. 1:18–36.

Daniels, Roger. 1962. *The Politics of Prejudice: The Anti-Japanese Movement in California and the Struggle for Japanese Exclusion.* Berkeley: Univ. of California Press.

Duberman, Martin, Martha Vicinus, and George Chauncey, eds. 1989. *Hidden from History: Reclaiming the Gay and Lesbian Past.* New York: New American Library.

Feagin, J., and C. Feagin. 1986. *Discrimination American Style: Institutional Racism and Sexism.* Englewood Cliffs, N.J.: Prentice-Hall.

Frankenstein, Marilyn. 1990. "Incorporating Race, Gender, and Class Issues in a Critical Mathematical Literacy Curriculum." *Journal of Negro Education.* 59, no. 3:336–47.

Freire, Paolo. 1970. *Pedagogy of the Oppressed.* New York: Herder and Herder.

Giddings, Paula. 1984. *When and Where I Enter: The Impact of Black Women on Race and Sex in America.* New York: Bantam Books.

Gill, Dawn, and Les Levidow, eds. 1987. *Anti-Racist Science Teaching.* London: Free Association Books.

Grauerholz, Elizabeth, and G. M. Scuteri. "Learning to Role-take: A Teaching Technique to Enhance Awareness of the 'Other.' " *Teaching Sociology* 17:480–83.

Griffin, Judith B. 1990. "Developing More Minority Mathematicians and Scientists: A New Approach." *Journal of Negro Education.* 59, no. 3:424–38.

Gwaltney, John Langston. l981. *Drylongso: A Self-Portrait of Black America.* New York: Vintage.

Hernandez, Hilda. 1989. *Multicultural Education: A Teacher's Guide to Content and Process.* Columbus, Ohio: Merrill.

Higginbotham, Elizabeth. 1988. *Integrating All Women into the Curriculum.* Memphis, Tenn.: Memphis State Univ., Center for Research on Women.

Hooks, Bell. 1994. *Teaching to Transgress: Education as the Practice of Freedom.* New York: Routledge.

Hudson, Brian. 1987. "Global and Multicultural Issues." *Mathematics Teaching* 119:52–55.

Ingram, James B. 1978. *Curriculum Integration and Lifelong Education.* UNESCO Division of Structures, Contents, and Methods of Education. New York: Pergamon.

Katz, Judith. 1978. *White Awareness: Handbook of Anti-Racist Training.* Norman: Univ. of Oklahoma Press.

Keefe, Susan, and A. Padilla. 1987. *Chicano Ethnicity.* Albuquerque: Univ. of New Mexico Press.

Kierstead, Diane. 1988. "Sex Role Stereotyping of College Professors: Bias in Students' Ratings of Instructors." *Journal of Education Psychology* 80, no. 3:342–44.

Kierstead, Diane. 1988. "Sex role stereotyping of college professors: bias in students' ratings of instructors." *Journal of Education Psychology* 80, no. 3:342–44.

Kitano, Harry, and R. Daniels. 1988. *Asian Americans.* Englewood Cliffs, N.J.: Prentice-Hall.

Knott, Elizabeth S. "Working with Culturally Diverse Learners." *Journal of Developing Education* 15, no. 2:14–18.

Konradi, Amanda. 1993. "Teaching About Sexual Assault: Problematic Silences and Solutions." *Teaching Sociology* 21, no. 1.

Lee, Janet. "Our Hearts Are Collectively Breaking." *Gender and Society* 3, no. 4:541–48.

Lee, Lee C. 1991. "The Opening of the American Mind: Educating Leaders for a Multicultural Society." *Human Ecology Forum* 19, 2–5.

Leung, Paul. 1990. "Asian-Americans and Psychology: Unresolved Issues." *Journal of Training and Practice in Professional Psychology* 4 no. 1:3–13.

Lin, Yi-guang. 1984. "The Use of Student Ratings in Promotion Decisions." *Journal of Higher Education* 55, no. 5:583–89.

Lorde, Audre. 1985. *I am Your Sister: Black Women Organizing Across Sexualities.* Latham, N.Y.: Kitchen Table/Women of Color Press.

Luke, Carmen, and Jennifer Gore. 1992. *Feminism and Critical Pedagogy.* New York: Routledge.

Martin, Elaine R. "Teacher Evaluation: A Selective Review of the Recent Literature." *Journal Classroom Interaction* 18, no. 2:16–19.

McDowell, Ceasar L. 1990. "The Unseen World: Race, Class, and Gender Analysis in Science Education Research." *Journal of Negro Education* 59, no. 3:273–91.

McIntosh, Peggy. 1991. "Interactive Phases of Curricular and Personal Revision with Regard to Race." In *Transforming the Curriculum: Ethnic Studies and Women's Studies,* edited by Johnella Butler and John Walter, Albany: SUNY Press.

McKay, Nellie Y. 1992. "A Troubled Peace: Black Women in the Halls of the White Academy." In *"Turning the Century": Feminist Theory in the 1990s,* edited by Glynis Carr, 21–37. Lewisburg, Pa.: Bucknell Univ. Press.

McKeachie, W. J. 1986. *Teaching Tips.* Lexington, Mass.: Heath.

Miller, Stuart. 1969. *The Unwelcome Immigrant: The American Image of the Chinese, 1785–1882.* Berkeley: Univ. of California Press.

Moraga, Cherrie, and Gloria Anzaldua, eds. 1983. *This Bridge Called My Back: Writing by Radical Women of Color.* New York: Kitchen Table/Women of Color Press.

Orenstein, Peggy. 1994. *SchoolGirls: Young Women, Self-Esteem, and the Confidence Gap.* New York: Doubleday.

Parmeter, Sara-Hope, and Irene Reti, eds. 1988. *The Lesbian in Front of the Classroom.* Santa Cruz, N.M.: McNaughton and Gunn.

Pharr, Suzanne. 1988. *Homophobia: A Weapon of Sexism.* Iverness, Calif.: Chardon Press.

Pheterson, Gail. 1986. "Alliances Between Women: Overcoming Internalized Oppression and Internalized Domination." *Signs: Journal of Women in Culture and Society* 12, no. 1:146–60.

Powell, Lois. 1990. "Factors Associated with the Underrepresentation of African Americans in Mathematics and Science." *Journal of Negro Education.* 59, no. 3:292–98.

Pruitt, A. S. 1984. "G*POP and the Federal Role in the Graduate Education of Minorities." *Journal of Negro Education* 53:106–13.

Pruitt, A. S., and P. D. Isaac. 1985. "Discrimination in Recruitment, Admission, and Retention of Minority Graduate Students." *Journal of Negro Education* 54:526–36.

Sanderson, Chela. 1990. "Feminism and Racism: A Report on the National Women's Studies Association Conference." In *Making Face/Making Soul,* edited by Gloria Anzaldua. San Francisco: Aunt Lute Foundation Books.

Schmitz, Betty. 1985. *Integrating Women's Studies into the Curriculum: A Guide and Bibliography.* Old Westbury, N.Y.: Feminist Press.

Serdahely, William and Georgia Ziemba. 1985. "Changing Homophobic Attitudes Through Sexuality Education." In *Bahers, Baiters and Bigots, Homophobia in American Society,* edited by John DeCecco. New York: Harrington Park Press.

Smith, Barbara. 1982. "Racism and Women's Studies." In *All the Women Are White, All the Blacks Are Men, But Some of Us Are Brave: Black Women's Studies,* edited by Barbara Smith. New York: Feminist Press, 1982.

Spanier, Bonnie, Alexander Bloom, and Darlene Boroviak, eds. 1984. *Toward a Balanced Curriculum: A Sourcebook for Initiating Gender Integration Projects.* Cambridge Mass.: Schenkman.

Spelman, Vicky. 1982. "Combating the Marginalization of Black Women in the ClassRoom." *Women's Studies Quarterly* 10, no. 2:15–16.

Stanfield-Potworowski. 1988. "Socializing Mathematics: ATM Easter Course 1988, Closing Lecture." *Mathematics Teaching* 125:3–8.

Staples, Robert. 1984. "Racial Ideology and Intellectual Racism: Blacks in Academia." *Black Scholar* 15, no. 2:2–17.

Takaki, Ronald. 1979. *Iron Cages: Race and Culture in Nineteenth Century America.* Seattle: Univ. of Washington Press.

Tan, Amy. 1989. *The Joy Luck Club.* New York: Putnam's.

Tobias, Sheila. 1978. *Overcoming Math Anxiety.* New York: Norton.

Toward a Balanced Curriculum: A Sourcebook for Initiating Gender Integration Projects. 1984. Cambridge, Mass.: Schenkman.

Toward a More Inclusive Curriculum. 1989. Gaithersburg, Md.: Ephemera/ Belles Lettres.

Van Geffen, Katherine. 1990. "Influence of Professor Gender and Perceived Use of Humor on Course Evaluation." *Humor* 3, no. 1:65–73.

Weis, Lois, ed. 1988. Class, Race, and Gender in American Education. Albany: SUNY Press.

Weis, Lois, and Michelle Fine, eds. 1993. *Beyond Silenced Voices: Class, Race and Gender in United States Schools.* Albany: SUNY Press.

12

Working with Students with Special Needs

BETHANY HEATON-CRAWFORD AND ERIC HOWES

More accurate and comprehensive assessment techniques, and better support services at the high school level, have resulted in more and more students with special needs reaching the college level. Nevertheless, it is still common for university faculty and staff to have little or no experience working with students with disabilities. This chapter is intended to provide you with a broad overview of some of the issues involved in providing academic support to such students. First, we briefly outline the different types of disabilities, and the laws that apply to these issues. Next, we provide examples of typical accommodations made for these students, as well as some suggestions for teaching modifications. The last section deals more specifically with issues and responsibilities regarding the accommodation of students with learning disabilities.

What do we mean by *disabilities?*

In this chapter, we will discuss two main types of disabilities: physical and learning. *Physical disabilities* take many forms, and how they are manifested varies greatly depending on the student's personality and the severity of impairment. The following are examples you might encounter: visual impairment, hearing impairment, cerebral palsy, brain injury, speech impairment, and carpal tunnel syndrome.

The second major type of disability is *learning disabilities* and associated disorders. Learning disabilities differ from physical disabilities

126

in two major ways: they are always invisible, and they tend to require more accommodation in terms of testing formats.

According to the National Joint Committee on Learning Disabilities:

> Learning disabilities is a general term that refers to a heterogeneous group of disorders manifested by significant difficulties in the acquisition and use of listening, speaking, reading, writing, reasoning, or mathematical abilities. These disorders are intrinsic to the individual, presumed to be due to central nervous dysfunction, and may occur across the life span. Problems in self-regulatory behaviors, social perception, and social interaction may exist with learning disabilities but do not by themselves constitute a learning disability. Although learning disabilities may occur concomitantly with other handicapping conditions (for example, sensory impairment, mental retardation, serious emotional disturbance) or with extrinsic influences (such as cultural differences, insufficient or inappropriate instruction), they are not the result of those conditions or influences. (NJCLD 1988)

This is only one of many official definitions. A more easily understandable one is that a learning disability is a permanent disorder affecting the manner in which a person of average to above-average intelligence takes in, processes, retains, and/or expresses information. If these definitions seem broad, that is intentional. Just as with physical disabilities, students who have learning disabilities experience them in differing ways and with differing severity. What is affected by their disability, and the way in which they differ from most other students, is how they process information. But it's also a matter of degree. In other words, we all have different strengths and weaknesses, but students with learning disabilities are affected to such a degree that their difficulties can impact substantially their ability to demonstrate what they know in a classroom setting. Here, again, are some examples: dyslexia, dysgraphia, language processing disorder, auditory processing deficit, visual processing deficit, and short/long-term memory deficits.

Two other conditions also affect a student's ability to process information. *Attention deficit disorder* is an associated disorder with some similarity to learning disabilities in terms of the modifications and accommodations needed to facilitate the learning processes of students who experience this disorder. Two variations of the disorder exist. The first is attention deficit disorder (ADD) without hyperactivity. Its predominant feature is a developmentally inappropriate and marked inattention to tasks. The second is attention deficit hyperactivity disorder (ADHD). Students with ADHD may be easily distracted by extraneous stimuli, blurt out answers to questions before you've finished asking them, and have difficulty remaining seated; in adolescents and older students, difficulty sitting still can develop into restlessness.

The second condition involves *psychiatric disabilities*, which can be expressed in a variety of ways. In general, psychiatric disorders are also invisible disabilities and will manifest themselves differently in each individual student. Certain behaviors sometimes appear and then disappear without apparent reason, due to the cyclical nature of the student's disability and/or medication being taken. The student's ability to stay awake or focused in class also can be affected by medication.

How will you know that a student has a disability?

Some disabilities are invisible, and some are more obvious. In all cases, it's best to create an open classroom environment in which students who have disabilities feel encouraged to come forward and identify themselves to you. You can do this in several ways, including a statement on the course syllabus, or an announcement in class. Here is a sample of a statement that could be used in either way: "If there is any student who needs special consideration due to a disability, please feel free to contact me during office hours or to set up an appointment so that we can work together to meet your academic needs."

Institutions have various ways of notifying faculty that students with disabilities are or will be in their classes. In many larger institutions, students themselves are responsible for notifying their instructors. Sometimes academic support service personnel who work with the students will notify faculty. The form such notification takes will vary from institution to institution. Determine what format your institution uses. In general, the notification will be written, confirming the disability and outlining the accommodations recommended for the particular difficulty, based on diagnostic testing and/or medical diagnosis. It is usually safe to assume that if the student has the notification/accommodation form, then they have met institutional requirements for assistance.

Students themselves usually are the best source of information about their own disability and how it is likely to affect them in your particular class. If the student has difficulty describing or knowing what he or she needs in your class, the academic support service personnel on campus are there to assist and serve as a resource both for you and the student.

What happens if the student has not notified the university but is asking for some accommodation?

In this case, refer the student to the office or personnel on campus designated to provide support to students with disabilities. You can usually find out where such support is by checking with your department, campus phone book, or human resources office.

What laws address what support services must be provided for students with disabilities at the postsecondary level?

Section 504 of the Rehabilitation Act of 1973 mandates that "no otherwise qualified handicapped individual in the United States shall, solely by reason of his handicap, be excluded from the participation in, be denied the benefits of, or be subjected to discrimination under any program or activity receiving federal financial assistance." According to the law, a handicapped person is one who has a "physical or mental impairment which substantially limits one or more major life activities." The definition includes people who have specific learning disabilities. The Rehabilitation Act also requires that faculty, administration, and staff be informed of the accommodations that must be made according to the law. In fact, faculty should receive this notification on a yearly or semester basis. Examples of information they should receive include:

• No student may be excluded from any course, or any courses of study, solely on the basis of a disability.

• Prohibitive rules, such as those banning tape recorders from the classroom, must be waived for some students with disabilities.

• Alternative testing and evaluation methods for measuring student achievement will be necessary for students with impaired sensory, manual, or speaking skills (except where those are the skills being measured).

• It is discriminatory to counsel students with disabilities toward more restrictive career options than students without disabilities, unless such counsel is based on strict licensing or certification requirements in a profession.

The Americans with Disabilities Act is modeled after the Rehabilitation Act of 1973 but extends its effect further into the public sector. The law prohibits segregation and discrimination against individuals with disabilities in the following areas: employment, public services, transportation, public accommodations, and telecommunications. It is intended to ensure that students with disabilities are further protected when they make the transition into the work world.

Specific university/college policies will vary by institution. Each institution should have a written policy outlining specifically how it will provide accommodations and support services to students with disabilities. Many times, such a policy has as its goal effective compliance with Section 504 of the Rehabilitation Act. Such policies should be circulated to departments and professors. If you have not received a copy of your institution's policy, you usually can get one from academic support service personnel.

What are some examples of support services a university/college provides?

The support services that institutions must provide include what we have been referring to as *accommodations* and *modifications*. Accommodations and modifications are those measures that provide individual students with disabilities access to all postsecondary activities. Accommodations and modifications are not intended to interfere with course objectives, but instead aim to allow students with disabilities to use their learning strengths to demonstrate the knowledge they have acquired. An institution also is required to provide sign language interpreters for students with hearing impairments; usually, such students will work directly with the appropriate academic support service personnel to arrange for interpreters. Tape recording lectures and/or being provided with note takers are two other typical accommodations. Students with hearing impairments, fine motor limitations (such as carpal tunnel, for example), and learning disabilities are examples of individuals who might need note takers or tape recorders. Tutoring often is provided to students with special learning needs, as well.

Alternative testing formats are another type of accommodation typically provided to students with disabilities. For example, students with visual impairments or learning disabilities in the area of reading comprehension or visual processing might have tests read to them. Another example would be providing students with learning disabilities extra time to complete an examination. In general, up to double the standard amount of time is allotted. This can help accommodate students taking somewhat longer to process information. Appropriate accommodations are determined on a case-by-case basis. What works for one student might not work for another.

Because students with learning disabilities have very specific academic needs, we focus in the rest of this chapter predominantly on accommodating those students; however, many of the approaches we will recommend apply to students with other types of disabilities too.

What are your responsibilities to the students with learning disabilities?

Any accommodations that you make as an instructor should not interfere with your objectives for the course. For example, if you are a writing instructor and you require students to demonstrate effective use of skills by developing a solid paper, then a student with disabilities cannot legitimately ask for a short-answer or outline alternative. However, you do have a responsibility to help students with disabilities develop those skills with the knowledge that it is an area of difficulty for them. Many cases are not as clear-cut as this example. What is important is that you try to help each individual student develop the skills required for the course in a way that utilizes his or her strengths. Oftentimes, the best way to determine appropriate accommodations is through negotiation. Accommodations and modifications are required, but what specific form that accommodation takes will vary both from course to course and from student to student. Remember, students with disabilities should be held just as accountable for their own learning as are other students. If they miss appointments or assignments, the consequences should be the same as for any other student.

Discretion and confidentiality. Some students with learning disabilities are very sensitive about being viewed as different from their peers. The best solution here is to take your cues from them. Your attitude and statements should let them know that you are receptive to their needs as learners. Even students who seem to be comfortable talking with you about their particular needs may not be comfortable with your discussing their special accommodations in front of their classmates. One way that you can maintain an open attitude without seeming to single out students with disabilities is by doing things for them that you would do for all students, such as encouraging students to use you as a resource during office hours. When students do come to office hours, make them comfortable by being patient when waiting for verbal responses, for example. In a team-teaching or a TA/professor situation, discuss with your colleague which of you is most suited to provide any accommodations.

Presentation of material. Many students with learning disabilities have difficulty processing information presented verbally; for such students, it's imperative that you make every effort to make your presentation and delivery as easy to process as possible. Below are some suggestions and teaching strategies to keep in mind. As you will see, most of the suggestions will help all students, whether or not they have disabilities.

A clear style of delivery, supplementing lectures and discussions with written notes, enunciating clearly while facing toward the class, and making sure each student can understand you are all critical. Students with processing disabilities or hearing impairments also can have difficulty with accents. If you have an accent, establish that your students are effectively processing the material you are presenting. For their part, students have a responsibility to communicate their needs to you. Often speaking more slowly can help, as can meeting with students later to clarify any information they missed.

What are your responsibilities to your department?

Awareness of students with disabilities, and expertise in meeting their special needs, varies from instructor to instructor. How accepting an instructor is also varies. Some still do not believe that learning disabilities exist or that academic accommodations should be made for students with such difficulties. The willingness to modify teaching methods and modes of evaluation to meet students' individual needs also varies considerably. In fact, it is sometimes difficult to differentiate students with learning disabilities from underachieving or poorly motivated students, especially without a comprehensive assessment. Because learning disabilities often have no visible manifestations, instructors often cannot distinguish a student with a learning disability from one who is simply unfocused or unmotivated, and they should not feel responsible to do so; that's a task best left up to the service provider.

Achieving your course objectives is your first responsibility. Any accommodations you provide should aim at reducing the impact of the specific disability, not at altering or "watering down" the curriculum in any way. Further, those course objectives need to remain the same for each student, regardless of his or her specific disability. However, you can modify the way you present material without altering its content. For example, if two students have disabilities affecting their writing processes, one might be allowed to supplement written responses with oral responses, the other to perform a short-answer test. Both students are still responsible for the content, but their alternative testing methods reduce the impact of the disability by focusing on their areas of strength. Legally, your responsibility is to provide "equivalent access" to the educational environment.

To get assistance in providing appropriate accommodations without changing course objectives, contact the service providers at your college or university. These service providers often will be familiar with the particular students and can provide advice regarding the delivery of academic support for each. They also serve as sources of information, including explanations of specific disabilities and your rights and responsibilities.

How do you balance your two sets of responsibilities?

Establishing effective communication between instructors and students, as well as taking advantage of resources available on campus, can often prevent problems from developing. At a meeting, with all parties present, each can voice concerns, and any areas of dispute are more easily reconciled. In a TA/professor situation, often the TA serves as liaison between the students with disabilities and professors. The objective is to reach a compromise while keeping in mind the goal of educating each and every student, regardless of any special needs. Think of things this way: you are helping students overcome their disability, not providing them with unfair advantages. The goal is to change the format of the course to meet the individual needs of each student, not to make the course easier for students with learning disabilities.

How do the needs of these students differ from those of students without learning disabilities?

When you view students with learning disabilities as having specific areas of strengths and weaknesses, you avoid labeling them as "disabled." In fact, taking this perspective, each and every student has areas of strength and areas of weakness; the only difference is that the students with specific processing deficits have placed themselves in environments that focus predominantly on the areas in which they are weak. Your awareness of there being different learning styles benefits every student you teach, and accommodating that variety often simply involves adopting good teaching techniques and practices.

These techniques include providing students repeated exposures to new or difficult information, and teaching to multiple modalities; both ensure that information is effectively communicated from instructor to student. Presenting information in different ways—be it auditory, visual, or kinesthetic—increases the chance that information will be presented in each student's area of strength, and be reviewed in those areas in which they are weak. The technique also can be used to reveal how different concepts relate to one another. Another good teaching practice that benefits students with special needs, as well as other learners, is to encourage and support meaningful and focused discussions whenever possible; such discussions allow students to actively participate in the learning process, and helps them to assimilate the information presented.

What about examinations and quizzes?

In dealing with students with disabilities, testing is typically an area of acute concern. A variety of accommodations are possible that do not modify exam format; these include time extensions, providing proctors and/or readers for exams, and providing separate locations free from distractions and undue stress. In cases where an evaluative format focuses on the area in which a student has difficulties, you may need to modify the existing exam format to better assess the student's knowledge. This can be done without changing the content covered on the exam or making the exam more or less difficult. This may involve replacing essay exams with short-answer or multiple-choice exams, objective exams for essay exams; allowing the student to supplement written answers with oral or taped responses; or any other modification that you and the student agree upon prior to the test. The important point is that the two of you need to communicate and develop a testing format that is both fair and allows the student to convey the information he or she has learned. In TA/professor situations, the burden of communicating often falls upon the teaching assistant, who should contact the support service office and become familiar with the student's particular needs.

What if a student with a learning disability does not notify you of his or her condition in advance? He or she should receive the same instruction and be evaluated in the same way as any other student in your class. Being notified of a disability after the student performs poorly on a test should not affect how you evaluate that test; however, once the student provides the appropriate accommodation form, you should provide the testing modifications from that point on.

What resources are available to help you meet each student's unique needs?

The most readily available resource is your university/college support service office; staff there should be able to answer any questions you have regarding the student and how best to deliver any accommodations and/or test modifications. They will have the student's documentation on file, and will be able to tell you how that particular student learns best, as well as how best to evaluate the student's progress. They will also be able to provide you with literature to answer any other questions.

What do you do if you suspect a student has a learning disability?

If you suspect that a student has an undiagnosed learning disability, you should refer the student to the academic support service office. If the student and counselor decide that it is warranted, the student will either be assessed by the institution's own staff or referred to a community-based testing site. However, sometimes a student can be helped to overcome his or her difficulties with easily administered minor modifications such as borrowing notes or being allowed extra time. This will save them the stress and financial burden of an outside evaluation. The evaluation provides students with strategies and recommendations for modifying their behavior in order to process information more effectively. The students may receive services only after they have official documentation. Often these written reports include specific recommendations regarding services the student will need at the postsecondary level.

As you can see, students with disabilities have specific learning styles that require some instructional accommodations and/or modifications. Such students are entitled by law to these accommodations and modifications, and yet they should be held just as accountable for their own learning as other students. They should be responsible for discussing their needs with their instructors in advance of the examination or classroom experience that will need to be modified. Your task is to address the individual needs of your students by establishing and maintaining open lines of communication and developing effective teaching practices.

13

Balancing Roles as Teacher, Student, and Person

SHARON HOLLENBACK AND MILENE MORFEI

One of the most daunting challenges you will face as a graduate student, especially if you have teaching responsibilities, will be figuring out how to balance the demands of your competing roles. Will the substantial time and energy your instructor and student roles require allow any room for a personal life? The answer is yes; however, accept now that keeping those roles in balance will be an ongoing struggle. When you decided to pursue a graduate degree, a commitment of perhaps several years, you began an exciting and potentially trying new chapter in your life. You were eager to continue to learn, not just through your own graduate work but also through your teaching. You've committed your several selves to a challenge. Right now you probably feel like a first-year student again in many ways, with all of the uneasiness of not knowing the "lay of the land," unsure about the location of campus buildings, what resources are available in the libraries, or even where to go for help. The hierarchy in your own department is still a mystery, and if you are prudent, you are avoiding any unwitting involvement in departmental politics. You may be particularly unsure about your immediate academic future, classes, research, facilities, professors.

As if these pressures of graduate student life are not enough, you also have been chosen to be a teaching assistant, which is both an honor and exciting opportunity. If your life plan includes an academic career, your teaching assistantship will lay a strong foundation for that professional future; even if your future does not now include academia, the experience garnered from your teaching responsibilities will prepare you for the career of your choice.

All of these new challenges are very exciting, and no doubt you are eager to get started. At the same time, you may be somewhat uneasy about how all the pieces are going to fit. How, you may be wondering, will you possibly be able to get everything done and done well? The answer lies in how you balance your various roles.

A Student First

Remember that you are a student first. Although your teaching assistantship is an important part of your academic experience, it is not the major reason you are in graduate school. The catch is that, although ideally your own work would come first, by taking an assistantship you have made a tremendous commitment to the undergraduates in your charge and to your teaching supervisor. You are a vital element in the academic mission of your university. Now you must find time for both your own work and your teaching duties. Organization and careful planning are imperative; set priorities and stick to them.

One important component in that planning will be the nature of your assistantship obligations. TA duties can range from grading and keeping office hours to full instructor responsibilities. What this means is that the time commitment will vary from assistantship to assistantship. If your assignment is lab supervision, for example, you will be required to be in the lab for a specific time period on particular days, and you will have to work around that schedule to get your own work done. Grading papers, in contrast, is an assignment that lends itself to a more flexible schedule.

Keep in mind that the time your TA responsibilities occupy will probably fluctuate around an average; at many universities they should average twenty hours a week. In one week you might spend just a few hours while in another week you might spend more than twenty hours. Try to attune yourself to the rhythm of the semester: building to the first paper, slowing down, then building again to midterms, and so on. Do some advance planning so you can take advantage of the "light" weeks to concentrate on your own coursework and research.

Generating a generic list of suggestions for balancing the instructor and graduate student roles is difficult, because each academic discipline, whether in sciences, arts, humanities, or professional schools, imposes its own unique demands. It is also true that each TA must find a system that works well for his or her personality and work style. However, one universal challenge faced by all graduate students and teaching assistants is how to balance their professional/academic lives with their personal lives.

Many graduate students feel that taking time for some semblance of a personal life is a luxury they cannot afford. The truth is, you *need* to take time for yourself even if you don't think you can. You need proper nutrition and exercise, and you need to relax (yes, relax!) occasionally. Constant work can be counterproductive. Spinning your wheels gets you nowhere fast, and ultimately your work suffers.

How you solve the challenge of carving out a personal life will depend on your individual circumstances. A married graduate student is more or less forced to have an existence outside the confines of academia; this is particularly true if he or she has children. But colleagues who ask married graduate students questions like "How do you do it?" don't realize that having a family is an asset, not a liability. Their very existence will help you maintain a personal life in spite of academia's inordinate demands on your time. The danger in being a single graduate student is that you have the "luxury" of spending all your time on academics. Don't do it! Force yourself to push the books away; your psychological well-being demands it. Grades should be a byproduct of your good effort but they need not be in and of themselves the driving force in your life.

Finally, accept that no matter how extraordinary your organizational skills there will be (many) times when your instructor, student, and person roles *will* get out of balance. An occasional imbalance is to be expected, but grab the reins before things spin too far out of control. Be self-assessing. Know when you need to ask for help, and where to get it. If you find yourself consistently spending more than twenty hours a week at your assistantship duties, talk with your teaching supervisor. If necessary, take up the matter with your graduate school. Resources exist on every campus to help you deal with the pressures of teaching, research, personal problems, and so on that could potentially throw you off course. Be proactive. Don't wait until you feel overwhelmed. Taking action to regain control over your life will itself lessen your stress level. Another way to regain a feeling of control might be to remind yourself that the path you are on is one that you have chosen. Focus on why you are in graduate school and on where that path will lead you. Put another way, even if you cannot actually change your situation, you can change the way you think about it.

The Best of Times

Accepting, even enjoying, the challenges of graduate school life could be the best way to not only survive but actually thrive. Graduate school will not last forever. Accept that to achieve your goal you'll have to live frugally for a time just as generations of students before you. Now professionals, they have proved it is possible to eat well *and* cheaply on pasta, beans, fruits, and vegetables, perhaps growing your own small garden to do so. Check out seasonal farmers' markets and come prepared with recipes from home. Watch for free events and activities in the community (concerts in the park, art exhibits, walks in the nature center). Scour thrift shops for clothes and furniture. Make the most of the opportunities available.

Take comfort knowing that most who have gone before you, survivors in the battle, now look back with fondness and nostalgia on their graduate school years. The learning is exciting. Certainly the frustration of the "hoops" that must be jumped through should be outweighed by the satisfaction of doing current, in-depth research in your chosen field. And the rewards are not exclusively intellectual; oftentimes, meaningful relationships are formed in graduate school mentorships, friendships, sometimes even life partnerships. It is gratifying when you realize you are the person responsible for a student really understanding a concept, writing an elegant paper, performing beyond even their expectations in an academic setting, or sharing your enthusiasm for, and commitment to, learning.

Think of graduate school as an adventure! Make every effort to enjoy what you are doing. Develop your sense of humor; do not take yourself too seriously. Get organized, do your best, ask for help before catastrophe strikes, be kind to yourself, and relish all the moments you can because you are off on a grand and glorious adventure. These times have the potential to be your best ever.

14

Becoming a Reflective Teacher

EMILY ROBERTSON AND ZEUS YIAMOUYIANNIS

What is Reflective Teaching?

How can I increase class participation?

Why did so many students fail the last exam?

Class went especially well today. What made the difference?

Is the amount and level of reading in this course appropriate for first year students?

My students don't seem very interested in the material I'm teaching. Is there anything I can do to make class more stimulating?

Questions such as these occur to all instructors. Everyone "reflects" to some extent about the success of their teaching. In this sense, no one needs to *become* a reflective teacher; it comes with the territory. Some instructors, however, certainly analyze their practice more than others, and some are more effective in finding useful answers to the questions they raise. Becoming a more reflective instructor involves expanding the depth and range of questions you ask about your own teaching. In addition, it means undertaking a more systematic study of your practice, which in turn will help you to improve instruction. It can also involve collaboration with others, including your own students, who have similar interests and questions.

In *The Reflective Practitioner*, Donald Schon (1983) draws a useful distinction between *reflection-in-action* and *reflection-on-action*. A competent practitioner learns to think on his or her feet and to improvise as he or she takes in new information or encounters the unexpected. This is what Schon calls reflection-in-action. He argues that these acts of improvisation take place within the framework of instructors' theories about teaching and learning and through interpretations of the roles of students and instructors, their values, and their understanding of institutional expectations about teaching and other factors. As instructors grow and develop and acquire advanced pedagogical expertise, these frameworks become better defined and more sophisticated, presenting instructors with a more versatile repertoire of reflection-in-action responses. For example, consider how two instructors may react to an unanticipated student response to a question. A more experienced instructor may try to discern what prompted the student's reply, while a second novice instructor may too quickly assume the student had not been paying attention.

Unlike reflection-in-action, reflection-on-action is usually done when you are not directly engaged in practice. In reflection-on-action, a practitioner reflects on tacit understandings and long held assumptions, subjecting them to scrutiny, with the aim of achieving deeper understandings of instructor and student roles, motivations and behaviors.

In Schon's theory, both types of reflection naturally lead to inquiry about student learning. For example, an instructor searching for the student's train of thought through reflection-in-action will typically formulate various hypotheses and try them out on the student. The instructor might ask questions such as: "Are you thinking . . . ," "Do you mean . . ." or "Do I understand you to say . . ." Then he or she will evaluate the student's response and if necessary probe some more. An instructor reflecting on action might rethink "bigger picture" issues about the nature of student instructor interaction. Do students have enough opportunity to interact with me and other students in my classroom? Is it always appropriate as an instructor to raise clarifying questions, or can I encourage other students to take on this role? In these cases, evaluating the results of the experiment is more complex, depending on the instructor's judgment of the success of the subsequent changes made in his or her teaching.

Expanding the Range of Reflection

While discussions of teaching often focus on student learning, there are other concerns. For example, have you made the best choice of themes and topics from the domain of the subject? Are your choices current, relevant to the students' concerns, and properly coordinated with related courses? What kinds of learning do you expect from your students: the acquisition of disciplinary knowledge and skills or the development of capacities for critical thinking, problem-solving, or effective communication? Do your readings, assignments, and methods of instruction reflect these choices?

Traditionally, instructors have been obligated to provide a syllabus that describes the course content, assignments, and methods of grading; to grade assignments in a timely fashion; to treat students with respect in the classroom; to be available for consultation; to determine grades fairly; and to give students an opportunity to evaluate their courses. Other chapters in this volume affirm these obligations, but they also ask you to consider additional ethical dimensions of your practice. For example, do female students receive equal opportunities for participation? Are your examples demeaning to any group? Do your examples encourage or reinforce sexism or racism? Are the contributions of different groups fairly represented in the readings? Do the students treat one another with respect? Do you in any way create an especially difficult environment for women or minorities or international students? It is important for you to reflect on these aspects of your teaching as well as those that instructors have traditionally considered.

Expanding the Depth of Reflection

The movement from reflection-in-action to reflection-on-action illustrates what it means to expand the depth of reflection: the instructor tries to identify and evaluate the assumptions that tacitly guide aspects of his or her practice. Consider the interpersonal dynamics among students in a particular class. One student continually tries to dominate the discussion. Some students appear arrogant or dismissive toward other students. The class grows impatient with one student's stream-of-consciousness replies to questions. Some are totally silent. Others use language some members of the class do not understand. Through countless episodes of reflection-in-action most instructors develop strategies for dealing with such situations. When one person is dominating the discussion instructors develop the ability to redirect questions and conversation to other members of the class. When necessary during discussion, instructors encourage students to clarify comments and to be sensitive toward the varied backgrounds and perspectives of other students. The instructor finds ways of getting students who have been silent to participate. These strategies become part of an instructor's repertoire and are automatically used in appropriate circumstances. They are the consequence of repeated reflection, experimentation, and evaluation.

Through reflection-on-action, the assumptions underlying these strategies can themselves be made the subject of reflection. For example, instructors who develop the strategies suggested above appear to be committed to equal participation by all students in classroom discussions. Is that always an appropriate objective? Do students have a right to not participate? How does the instructor properly acknowledge cultural variations in norms concerning public speech? For example, what if a student correctly supposes that his or her views will be rejected by other students and he or she will be stigmatized? Or does it matter that the usual norms of classroom discussion (e.g., the challenging of each other's ideas) may be more comfortable for some groups than for others?

One assumption the instructor makes in using the aforementioned strategies is that the responsibility for controlling the discussion rests entirely with him or her. Is it ever appropriate for the instructor to share that responsibility with the students? Should the instructor check whether his or her description of a given situation matches that of the students? Do the other students resent the talkative student for dominating the discussion or do they appreciate his or her ability to raise questions others had but were unable to articulate? Is the student admired for being willing to risk submitting his or her views to public scrutiny or for challenging the instructor's ideas?

Reflection-on-action can generate alternatives to your present assumptions which in turn generate new possibilities for actions that might improve instruction. Some instructors believe that students should be involved in the evaluation of the instructional process throughout the course, rather than only at the end. These instructors include the students in the process of reflection as a way of increasing the effectiveness of their teaching, as a way of making students responsible for their own learning.

Teacher Research

The above descriptions of reflection suggest the importance of research to reflection. Raising questions about your practice and formulating hypotheses about how to improve it will not be useful unless it is possible to evaluate those hypotheses. Thus, reflective teaching requires engaging in systematic study of your own instruction, doing research in your own classrooms, and collecting data that will permit you to judge the success of your experiments.

Classroom research may not meet all of the same standards as inquiry you conduct in your role as a researcher in your discipline, but it does require some form of data collection. The types of data might include: student responses to a question you ask in class which can then be used to judge the effectiveness of a particular session; student interviews about the problems they're having with the class and suggestions for change; student journal entries about classroom interactions; teaching portfolios; videotapes of classes; colleagues' comments about a classroom observation; samples of student work; or student opinion questionnaires. Other chapters in this book offer helpful suggestions concerning methods for collecting and analyzing data, such as videotaping classes, making use of assessment techniques, and developing portfolios. Another helpful reference on this subject is *Classroom Assessment Techniques: A Handbook for the College Teacher* by Tom Angelo and K. Patricia Cross.

Teacher research can be conducted individually or by groups of instructors with similar interests and questions. There is growing interest in collaborative research at the elementary, secondary, and post-secondary level (Cochran-Smith and Lytle 1993 and Schratz 1990).

The Challenges and Benefits of Reflective Teaching

As you experiment and integrate newly acquired insights and skills, your teaching competence might initially appear to decline. When new approaches fail you might wonder why you ever deserted the "tried and true." If you decide to collaborate you might feel uncomfortable disclosing your problems to another instructor, particularly if he or she has more experience or status than you. Your students and other instructors may see your efforts to improve as weakness. Cochran-Smith and Lytle (1993, 87) note that "teachers are not encouraged to talk about classroom failures. . . . The occupational culture perpetuates the myth that good teachers rarely have questions that they cannot answer about their own practices."

Most instructors find that the benefits of reflective teaching are substantial. Reflection makes teaching more enjoyable and more intellectually satisfying. Collaboration with other instructors breaks down the isolation of the typical classroom. For new instructors reflective teaching offers a way of answering questions and reducing anxiety. For experienced instructors it can be a source of renewal and a means of overcoming burn-out. Problems seem less like failures and more like opportunities for learning. Reflective teaching offers the promise of increased learning for both you and your students.

15

Building a Professional Portfolio

LEO M. LAMBERT

Elsewhere in this volume, you have been urged to become a reflective teacher. Being a reflective teacher means that you are prepared to deal with the "big questions" of teaching, which on the surface can seem deceptively simple. These questions include:

• Am I an effective teacher? How do students perceive my teaching strengths and weaknesses? How do my peers regard my teaching?

• How can I improve my course to enhance student learning?

• How do I know I am reaching my students? Are they really learning the important concepts?

• Are my exams and class assignments fair and appropriate? Do I provide students with adequate and helpful feedback?

One way to begin to answer these and other important questions is to use a portfolio to facilitate the collection and interpretation of evidence about your teaching and other key aspects of professional life.

A professional portfolio is simply a collection of physical evidence that helps document and describe your professional accomplishments. Portfolios can be very useful in encouraging your systematic collection of evidence of professional development over time and in promoting reflection about your professional growth. In academe, professional portfolios usually contain evidence pertaining to all facets of one's career, including research and creative accomplishments, teaching accomplishments, and service contributions. The following table provides examples of the kinds of evidence that might be collected under each of these categories.

Possible Evidence for Inclusion in Portfolios

Evidence About Teaching Accomplishment	Evidence About Research and Creative Accomplishments	Evidence About Service Contributions
written classroom observation reports from faculty supervisors	a description of past and future agendas pertaining to scholarly research and creative accomplishments	descriptions of service to university and departmental committees
videotapes of classroom teaching	sample reprints or preprints of published articles or book chapters	notations of participation in university governance
course/lab/recitations section syllabi	notations of research presented at conferences of scholarly/disciplinary societies	notations of administrative service to department, college, or university
a self reflective statement about teaching philosophy and personal teaching goals	peer reviews of scholarly/creative work	notations of community service related to university position
mid-course student evaluations	notices of juried exhibitions	notations of service to local schools
end-of-course student evaluations	evidence of service to an academic society as a journal editor, manuscript reviewer, or conference paper reviewer	notations of service to professional/disciplinary society or organization
notations of teaching awards and recognitions	notations of honors and recognitions in research and creative endeavors	
special teaching-related projects, materials, or curriculum authored	evidence of external funding secured to conduct research	
descriptions of courses previously taught (or that one is qualified to teach)	descriptions of service as a peer reviewer for research grant competitions	
sample student essays, papers, and class projects	evidence of your mentoring of apprentices in research and creative endeavors who have gone on to achieve success of their own	
written reflections of teaching evaluations		
unsolicited testimony from students		
evidence of participation in teaching-related sessions at conferences and disciplinary society meetings		
a summary statement from a faculty mentor		

Seven Principles of Portfolio Development

Beginning a Professional Portfolio: Deciding Upon Its Primary Purpose

There are two primary purposes for developing a teaching portfolio. The first is simply to stimulate professional development and improvement. In the literature on educational evaluation, the term "formative evaluation" is often used to describe the collection and analysis of data for the purpose of improving a program, curriculum, or individual instruction. Developing a portfolio for professional development purposes means that *you* are the primary person responsible for the evaluation and interpretation of the evidence contained in it (although you certainly could elect to discuss and interpret the evidence with a mentor or peer).

The second primary purpose for developing a portfolio is to inform a personnel decision, such as a hiring, reappointment, promotion, or tenure decision. This is often termed "summative evaluation" because a summary decision is being made about an individual person based on the evidence in his or her portfolio. In these cases, the primary audience for the portfolio are key decision makers, who will take the final personnel action, such as a hiring committee, the department chair, or a promotion and tenure committee.

One of the first decisions you should make before beginning your portfolio is to determine the purpose for its development, because that purpose will determine the nature of the evidence you place in it. For example, a faculty member might develop a portfolio for formative purposes because she is contemplating major revisions to her large introductory course and she wishes to use evidence from her portfolio to inform the new course design. Thus, she might elect to collect the following types of data: student evaluations from her present introductory course; analysis of course assignments for the past several semesters; analysis of her present course syllabus; and data about how students succeed in subsequent courses in the department. In contrast, portfolios developed for summative purposes might be prescribed to include certain kinds of evidence. For example, a TA being considered for reappointment might be required by her department chair to submit a videotape of her teaching, end-of-semester student evaluations, and a short self-analysis of her strengths and areas for development as an instructor. As another illustration, a senior graduate student applying for a faculty position at a small liberal arts college that prizes excellent teaching would do well to be sure to provide clear evidence of demonstrated teaching effectiveness and a true commitment to that dimension of academic life.

Remember, purpose determines evidence!

Academic and Professional Goals Should Drive Portfolio Development

The content of the portfolio should reflect your academic and professional goals. In fact, your academic and professional goals should drive your portfolio development. While this point might seem self-evident, acting on it is crucial to preparing a portfolio that represents you honestly and fairly. Consider the following examples: in the case of junior faculty members at research universities preparing portfolios for promotion and tenure decisions, it is paramount that they first understand the criteria upon which those promotion and tenure decisions will be based. Because scholarly research will likely count heavily (at least 50 percent), at least 50 percent of the portfolio should reflect this important emphasis. In the case of a graduate student aiming for a career at a liberal arts college where innovative teaching is prized, it would be wise for him or her to gain (and document) as much teaching experience as possible and search for opportunities that will allow for innovative experimentation.

Remember, set your academic and professional goals first. A portfolio is simply a vehicle to help you achieve those goals.

Begin Collecting Evidence Early and Systematically

For many faculty and graduate students, the challenge of collecting far-flung materials and evidence for inclusion in the portfolio seems daunting. Two graduate students in philosophy at Syracuse University, Greg Ganselle and David Woodruff, have metaphorically described the process of dealing with professional portfolio contents as "files and piles." In the broadest sense, the entire contents of an instructor's filing cabinets are fair game for inclusion in the professional portfolio, including collections of syllabi, examinations, student evaluations, reprints of research papers, and so on. Again, the challenge is to sort and winnow down these files into "piles" of materials that portray the appropriate balance of professional accomplishments. To encourage graduate students to begin collecting materials early on in their academic careers, the TA Program at Syracuse University, for example, provides each new TA with an expandable, accordion file in which to begin building his or her professional portfolio collection.

Practical Ways to Begin Collecting Teaching Evidence

Most new graduate teaching assistants have very little if any prior teaching experience and often ask a very basic question about collecting evidence for their portfolios: How can I plan my teaching so that I can collect materials for my portfolio even during my first semester of teaching? The following exercises can provide you with valuable information about your teaching and are relatively easy to arrange. You might wish to try all of them, even during your first year of teaching.

• Find a partner who is willing to videotape your class or recitation section and then spend two hours with you reviewing the videotape and offering constructive feedback and comment. Write up some informal notes about your experience, and then place both the videotape and the notes in your portfolio. (Be sure to offer reciprocal services to your partner!)

• Try using a mid-course evaluation instrument to gauge your students' opinions about how your class, studio, recitation section, or lab is progressing. You might use a form similar to Syracuse University's Teaching Assistant/Associate Mid-Course Feedback Form (see appendix A), or you can simply ask your students to take out a piece of paper and offer you their narrative comments and opinions. Consider the information provided by the students on your own, and then discuss any important implications informally with your faculty supervisor or a more experienced peer. Write a reflective summary comment and place it, along with the student comments, in your portfolio.

• Place a copy of your course, lab, studio, or recitation section syllabus in your portfolio for safekeeping. Occasionally write notes on the syllabus about what you would change the next time you teach that same course. Later, add a copy of the new syllabus to your portfolio for comparison and write a brief reflective statement on the reasons for the changes in the syllabus.

• Ask your faculty supervisor to make at least one visit to your classroom, studio, or lab during the semester, and then arrange to discuss his or her observations. Your supervisor may be willing to write a brief report (one page) detailing his or her reactions, comments, and suggestions, which you can then add to your portfolio. (This is standard procedure in some departments and is almost always approached as a supportive, improvement-oriented exercise!)

• Keep copies of some student works. (You should ask the students' permission to include their work in your portfolio.) For example, you might keep a copy of both the draft of a student's paper with your comments about how it might be strengthened and a copy of the final graded paper. You might also include a sample lab exercise that you designed, an examination you constructed, or a group project assignment that you invented.

• Include examples of your class assignments. Attach an analysis of student performance on the assignments and how you responded to the student's work.

• Begin the practice of using your department's standard end-of-semester teaching evaluation instrument. (These are usually optically scanned and computer scored.) The data is particularly helpful when it's kept longitudinally. Again, make some reflective notes about your reaction to the aggregate analysis, particularly offering insight about any unusual student responses to questions.

• Keep a page of notes in preparation for writing a reflective statement of your teaching philosophy that you eventually will include as a key component of your portfolio. While you might not draft that statement for a year or two, your notes about your emerging thinking about your philosophy of teaching will be very helpful to you later on.

While this list of ideas might appear daunting at first, all of the activities can be scheduled easily over the course of the year with advance planning on your part. Most important, you'll learn a great deal about yourself as an instructor and be glad later on that you took the time to collect important evidence about your professional growth.

Develop Different Portfolios to Suit the Needs of Various Audiences

Portfolios come in many shapes and forms: a banker's box full of files, videotapes, books, and journal reprints; a three-ring binder divided into several sections; or an accordion file of materials. It could soon become commonplace for multimedia portfolios to be developed in digital form; some instructors have already begun to experiment with the use of hypertext for organizing their electronic portfolios.

Whatever the format, one size portfolio does not necessarily fit all purposes. Consider the faculty hiring committee responsible for screening two hundred applications for a single position. Most small committees could not begin to examine full-blown portfolios for each candidate. In this instance, a candidate aiming to emphasize his teaching excellence, for example, might supplement his curriculum vitae with a very distilled version of his portfolio, including a one-or two-page philosophical statement about teaching, a one-page summary of teaching evaluations, and a table of contents to the larger portfolio indicating that other materials are available upon request. A promotion and tenure committee, on the other hand, would very likely expect to examine a very extensive version of a professional portfolio in conjunction with its review.

Whatever the size, careful organization of the portfolio is key. A well-planned table of contents is very useful to readers in directing them to materials of special interest. Again, especially for personnel decision making purposes, accompanying your portfolio selections with an annotated listing of materials not included in the portfolio but available upon request not only demonstrates to the reader that a broader portfolio is available, but that you have taken the time to carefully select those portfolio elements most germane to the decision at hand.

The Process Is More Important Than the Product

It is easy to lose perspective in developing a professional portfolio and become preoccupied with the end product—the physical portfolio—itself. In actuality, the process of portfolio development may be more useful than the final product. The process of portfolio development will cause you to reflect on academic and professional goals; assess your strengths and areas needing further development; and experiment with means to gather important data about your professional accomplishments, such as videotaping a class session or writing a reflective statement about your teaching philosophy.

Of equal importance, portfolios promote dialogue about professional development with colleagues and mentors. All too often in academe conversations about subjects as essential as teaching receive short shrift, if they occur at all. Portfolios can be enormously useful for promoting more regular conversations about teaching and other aspects of professional life. Importantly, these conversations will be informed by evidence rather than constrained by old prejudices.

Level	Purpose of Portfolio
Early graduate school	Stimulate the collection of evidence about teaching and research accomplishments
	Promote reflection about initial teaching and other professional experiences
	Encourage discussion about professional activities with faculty mentors
Late graduate school	Stimulate thinking about a philosophy of teaching and a future research agenda
	Assist in the academic job hunt
	Assist in the non-academic job hunt
Pretenure years	Facilitate promotion review
	Facilitate tenure review
	Encourage discussion about professional growth with colleagues, department chairs, and deans
Posttenure years	Encourage reflection about professional growth throughout one's academic career
	Facilitate posttenure review

Time and time again, graduate students have reported that the best aspect of preparing a portfolio was the opportunity it gave them for extended conversations with their faculty mentors about their goals, aspirations, and accomplishments. Graduate students also consistently report that it is just this type of reflective retrospection that best prepared them for interviewing for their first faculty positions.

Portfolios Have Utility at Every Stage of an Academic Career

Portfolios are used today by a wide range of scholars, from graduate students just beginning doctoral programs to senior, tenured faculty members. The table above demonstrates how the purpose of the portfolio can shift with each new professional level attained.

At each stage, portfolio development can help scholars reflect on their past achievements and activities, chart future professional goals, and provide selective documentation to decision makers (promotion and tenure committees, hiring committees, etc.).

As a graduate student, it is your responsibility to begin thinking about your portfolio as early as possible in your university career. An investment of your time in a professional portfolio is an investment in your professional future and in the formation of meaningful and substantive relationships with mentors and peers in your department with whom you will chart your plans for professional development.

Appendix
Works Cited
Index

#20104-0018U   ■■■■   NCS Trans-Optic® ED01-14758 :105   A2403

Teaching Associate/Teaching Assistant Mid-Course Feedback

TESTING SERVICES

SYRACUSE UNIVERSITY

MAKE YOUR MARKS HEAVY AND DARK.

USE NO. 2 WOODEN PENCIL ONLY.

EXAMPLE

A B C D E F G H I J
① ● ③ ④ ⑤ ⑥ ⑦ ⑧ ⑨ ⑩

ERASE COMPLETELY WHEN NECESSARY

Please complete the following information:

Course Name: _____

Course Prefix and Number: _____

Section Number: _____

TA: _____

Please respond to the following questions by darkening the numbered circle to the right that best represents your response.

(1) strongly disagree   (2) disagree   (3) neutral   (4) agree   (5) strongly agree   (6) not applicable

The TA:

1. prepares well for class. (1.)
2. makes oral presentations clearly. (2.)
3. presents material in an organized fashion. (3.)
4. encourages questions. (4.)
5. responds well to questions. (5.)
6. provides helpful feedback on course assignments. (6.)
7. shows concern that you are learning the material. (7.)
8. makes him/herself available outside of class. (8.)
9. demonstrates knowledge of the subject matter. (9.)
10. presents new material in an understandable way. (10.)
11. shows a willingness to help students having difficulty. (11.)
12. communicates concepts, content, and issues clearly. (12.)
13. is approachable about course related questions. (13.)
14. shows enthusiasm for the subject and for teaching. (14.)
15. Optional question #1 (15.)
16. Optional question #2 (16.)
17. Optional question #3 (17.)
18. Optional question #4 (18.)
19. Optional question #5 (19.)

Over, please =>

159

SIDE 2 **Open Ended Questions**

A B C D E F G H I J
① ② ③ ④ ⑤ ⑥ ⑦ ⑧ ⑨ ⑩

A B C D E F G H I J
① ② ③ ④ ⑤ ⑥ ⑦ ⑧ ⑨ ⑩

20. What strengths has the TA demonstrated that help you to learn the course material?

A B C D E F G H I J
① ② ③ ④ ⑤ ⑥ ⑦ ⑧ ⑨ ⑩

A B C D E F G H I J
① ② ③ ④ ⑤ ⑥ ⑦ ⑧ ⑨ ⑩

A B C D E F G H I J
① ② ③ ④ ⑤ ⑥ ⑦ ⑧ ⑨ ⑩

A B C D E F G H I J
① ② ③ ④ ⑤ ⑥ ⑦ ⑧ ⑨ ⑩

A B C D E F G H I J
① ② ③ ④ ⑤ ⑥ ⑦ ⑧ ⑨ ⑩

A B C D E F G H I J
① ② ③ ④ ⑤ ⑥ ⑦ ⑧ ⑨ ⑩

21. What specific ways could the TA improve how he or she teaches this course?

A B C D E F G H I J
① ② ③ ④ ⑤ ⑥ ⑦ ⑧ ⑨ ⑩

A B C D E F G H I J
① ② ③ ④ ⑤ ⑥ ⑦ ⑧ ⑨ ⑩

A B C D E F G H I J
① ② ③ ④ ⑤ ⑥ ⑦ ⑧ ⑨ ⑩

A B C D E F G H I J
① ② ③ ④ ⑤ ⑥ ⑦ ⑧ ⑨ ⑩

A B C D E F G H I J
① ② ③ ④ ⑤ ⑥ ⑦ ⑧ ⑨ ⑩

A B C D E F G H I J
① ② ③ ④ ⑤ ⑥ ⑦ ⑧ ⑨ ⑩

22. What other comments would you like to make regarding the TA or the course?

A B C D E F G H I J
① ② ③ ④ ⑤ ⑥ ⑦ ⑧ ⑨ ⑩

A B C D E F G H I J
① ② ③ ④ ⑤ ⑥ ⑦ ⑧ ⑨ ⑩

A B C D E F G H I J
① ② ③ ④ ⑤ ⑥ ⑦ ⑧ ⑨ ⑩

A B C D E F G H I J
① ② ③ ④ ⑤ ⑥ ⑦ ⑧ ⑨ ⑩

A B C D E F G H I J
① ② ③ ④ ⑤ ⑥ ⑦ ⑧ ⑨ ⑩

A B C D E F G H I J
① ② ③ ④ ⑤ ⑥ ⑦ ⑧ ⑨ ⑩

**TESTING
SERVICES**

**SYRACUSE
UNIVERSITY**

(OER/TS 9/94)   **(DO NOT WRITE BELOW THIS LINE)**

Works Cited

AAHE Assessment Forum. 1992. "Principles of Good Practice for Assessing Learning." Washington, D.C.: American Association for Higher Education.

Allen, Paula Gunn. 1990. *Spider Women's Granddaughters: Traditional Tales and Contemporary Writing by Native American Women.* New York: Fawcett Columbine.

American Psychiatric Association. 1987. *Diagnostic and Statistical Manual of Mental Disorders.* 3d ed. rev. Washington, D.C.: American Psychiatric Association, 1987.

Angelo, Thomas A. 1991. "Ten Easy Pieces: Assessing Higher Learning in Four Dimensions." In *Classroom Research: Early Lessons from Success.* New Directions for Teaching and Learning, no. 46. San Francisco: Jossey-Bass.

Angelo, Thomas A., and K. Patricia Cross. 1993. *Classroom Assessment Techniques: A Handbook for the College Teacher.* 2d ed. San Francisco: Jossey-Bass.

Anzaldua, Gloria. 1987. *Borderlands/La Frontera.* San Francisco: Spinsters/Aunt Lute.

Bandura, A. 1982. "Self-Efficacy Mechanism in Human Agency." *American Psychologist* 37, no. 2:122–47.

Belenky, Mary Field, Blythe McVicker, Nancy Rule Goldberger, Jill Mattuck Tarule. 1986. *Women's Ways of Knowing.* New York: Basic Books.

Berthoff, Ann. 1982. *Forming, Thinking, Writing: The Composing Imagination.* Montclair, N.J.: Boynton Cook.

Britton, James. 1993. *Language and Learning: The Importance of Speech in Children's Development.* 2d ed. Portsmouth, N.H.: Boynton Cook.

Brophy, J. 1987. "Synthesis of Research on Strategies for Motivating Students to Learn." *Educational Leadership* 47, no. 2:40–48.

Brown, Rita Mae. 1977. *Rubyfruit Jungle.* New York: Bantan.

Centra, J., R. Froh, P. Gray, and Leo M. Lambert. 1987. *Evaluating Teaching for Promotion and Tenure.* Acton, Mass.: Copley Press.

Cochran-Smith, Marilyn, and Susan L. Lytle. 1993. *Inside/Outside: Teacher Research and Knowledge.* New York: Teachers College Press.

Crane, Diana. 1972. *Invisible Colleges: Diffusion of Knowledge in Scientific Communities.* Chicago: Univ. of Chicago Press.

Cross, K. Patricia. 1983. "On College Teaching." *Journal of Engineering Education.* January, 9–14.

———. 1990. "Classroom Research: Helping Professors Learn More About Teaching and Learning." In *How Administrators Can Improve Teaching,* edited by Peter Seldin and Associates. San Francisco: Jossey-Bass.

Csikszentmihalyi, M. 1975. *Beyond Boredom and Anxiety: The Experience of Plan in Work and Games.* San Francisco: Jossey-Bass.

———. 1978. "Intrinsic Rewards and Emergent Motivation." In *The Hidden Costs of Reward,* edited by M. R. Lepper and D. Greene. Hillsdale, N.J.: Erlbaum.

Duplechan, Larry. 1986. *Blackbird.* New York: St. Martin's Press.

Dweck, C. S. 1986. "Motivational Processes Affecting Learning." *American Psychologist* 41, no. 10:1040–48.

Edgerton, R., P. Hutchings, and K. Quinlan. 1991. *The Teaching Portfolio: Capturing the Scholarship in Teaching.* Washington, D.C.: American Association for Higher Education.

Edwards, Harry. 1980. *The Struggle That Must Be.* New York: Macmillan.

Feldman, Kenneth A. 1976. "The Superior College Teacher from the Students' View." *Research in Higher Education* 5:43–88.

Froh, R., P. Gray, and Leo M. Lambert. 1994. "The Professional Portfolio." In *Recognizing Faculty Work: Reward Systems for the Year 2000,* edited by R. Diamond and B. Adams. New Directions in Higher Education, no. 81, San Francisco: Jossey-Bass.

Garza, Hisauro. 1993. "Second-Class Academics: Chicano/Latino Faculty in U.S. Universities." *New Directions for Teaching and Learning* 53:33–41.

Geertz, Clifford. 1983. *Local Knowledge.* New York: Basic Books, 1983.

Gere, Ann Ruggles, ed. 1985. *Roots in the Sawdust: Writing to Learn Across the Disciplines.* Urbana, Ill.: NCTE.

Hamill, D. D., J. E. Leigh, G. McNutt, and S. C. Larsen. 1981. "A New Definition of Learning Disabilities." *Learning Disabilities Quarterly,* 4, no. 4, 336–42.

Hegel, George. 1967. *Phenomenology of Mind.* Translated by J. B. Baillie. New York: Harper.

Hoffman, Banesh. 1972. *Albert Einstein: Creator and Rebel.* New York: New American Library, 1972.

Keller, J. M. 1983. "Motivational Design of Instruction." In *Instructional-Design Theories and Models: An Overview of Their Current Status,* edited by C. M. Reigeluth. Hillsdale, N.J.: Erlbaum.

———. 1987. "Strategies for Stimulating the Motivation to Learn." *Performance and Instruction* 26, no. 8:1–7.

Kelly, Diana K. 1993. "Classroom Assessment for Adult Learners." Paper presented at Classroom Research Institute, 11–14 August, Univ. of California, Berkeley.

Kelly, Diana K., Michelle Miller, and Michelle Wilder. 1991. "Increasing Involvement in Learning with Classroom Assessment." In *Knowing: The Power of Stories,* edited by Philip H. Dreyer. Fifty-fifth Yearbook of the Claremont Reading Conference.

Knoblach, C. H., and Lil Brannon. 1982. "On Students' Rights to Their Own Texts: A Model of Teacher Response." *College Composition and Communication* 33:157–66.

Konradi, Amanda. 1993. "Teaching About Sexual Assault: Problematic Silences and Solutions." *Teaching Sociology* 21, no. 1.

Kuhn, Thomas. 1970. *The Structure of Scientific Revolutions.* Chicago: Univ. of Chicago Press, 1970.

Lempriere, J. N.d. *A Classical Dictionary: Containing a Copious Account of All the Proper Names Mentioned in the Ancient Authors; with the Value of Coins, Weights, and Measures, Used Among the Greeks and Roman: and a Chronological Table.* New and Complete Edition. London: Milner and Sowerby.

Moody, Anne. 1968. *Coming of Age in Mississippi.* New York: Dial.

Morrison, Toni. 1987. *Beloved.* New York: New American Library.

Mosteller, F. 1989. "The 'Muddiest Point in the Lecture' as a Feedback Device." *On Teaching and Learning: The Journal of the Harvard-Danforth Center* 3:10–21.

Oakes, Jeannie. 1990. "Opportunities, Achievement, and Choice: Women and Minority Students in Science and Mathematics." In *Review of Research in Education* Vol. 16, ed. Courtney B. Cazden, 153–222. American Education Research.

Pintrich, Paul R. 1988. "A Process Oriented View of Student Motivation and Cognition." In *Improving Teaching and Learning Through Research,* edited by J. S. Stark and L. A. Mets. New Directions for Institutional Research, no. 57. San Francisco: Jossey-Bass.

Porter, L. W., and E. E. Lawler. 1968. *Managerial Attitudes and Performance.* Homewood, Ill.: Irwin.

Rowe, M. B. 1987. "Wait Time: Slowing Down May Be a Way of Speeding Up." *American Educator,* 11, no. 1, 38–43, 47.

Sandler, Bernice R. 1989. *The Restoration of Title IX: Implications for Higher Education.* Washington, D.C.: Association of American Colleges.

Schoem, D. L., L. Frankel, X. Zuniga, and E. A. Lewis. 1993. *Multicultural Teaching in the University.* Westport, Conn.: Praeger.

Schon, Donald A. 1983. *The Reflective Practitioner: How Professionals Think in Action.* New York: Basic.

Schratz, Michael. 1990. "Researching While Teaching: A Collaborative Action Research Model to Improve College Teaching." *Journal on Excellence in College Teaching* 1:98–108.

Sherman, T. M., L. P. Armistead, F. Forest, M. A. Barksdale, and G. Reif. 1987. "The Quest for Excellence in University Teaching." *Journal of Higher Education* 58, no. 1:66–81.

Walker, Alice. 1982. *The Color Purple*. New York: Harcourt Brace Jovanovich.

Wlodkowski, R. J. 1991. *Enhancing Adult Motivation to Learn*. San Francisco: Jossey-Bass.

Young, Art, and Toby Fulwiler, eds. 1986. *Writing Across the Disciplines: Research into Practice*. Boston: Boynton/Cook.

Young, M. 1982. "Increasing Learner Participation." *Performance and Instruction* 21, no. 4:7–10.

Zemke, R., and S. Zemke. 1981. "Thirty Things We Know for Sure About Adult Learning." *Training: The Magazine of Human Resources Development* 18, no. 6:45–52.

Index